Rampage by Firestorm

A Season for Disaster

Rampage by Firestorm

A Season for Disaster

Robert W. Sisk

sweetgrassbooks
an imprint of Farcountry Press

Library of Congress Control Number: 2024901676

ISBN 978-1-59152-340-6

Design by Sue Murray

Front cover: Corona Borealis Studio/Shutterstuck.com
Back cover: Pong Ch/Shutterstock.com

For more information or to order extra copies of this book call Farcountry Press toll free at (800) 821-3874 or visit www.farcountrypress.com

sweetgrassbooks
an imprint of Farcountry Press

Produced by Sweetgrass Books

PO Box 5630, Helena, MT 59604; (800) 821-3874; www.sweetgrassbooks.com.

Produced and printed in the United States of America

28 27 26 25 24   1 2 3 4 5

In memory of my wonderful wife, Rodna (Roddy)
and
A special tribute to the ultimate firefighter,
Samuel E. Sisk, Peoria, IL, Fire Department (Ret.)

Contents

Chapter 1: Entering the Season 1
Chapter 2: Tragedy on the Selway. 3
Chapter 3: The Accident Investigation 15
Chapter 4: The Engines Investigation 36
Chapter 5: Engine Serial Number 141621 44
Chapter 6: Cook Creek Ridge 53
Chapter 7: Mortar Creek Fire 64
Chapter 8: Harrah's Lodge 78
Chapter 9: Blowup on the West Side 80
Chapter 10: Sorrow on Storm King Mountain 85
Chapter 11: Mobilizing for Battle 89
Chapter 12: Reinforcements and Battling the Fire 96
Chapter 13: Blowup, Entrapment, and Escape 99
Chapter 14: Aftermath 108
Chapter 15: Conclusion and Findings. 111
Chapter 16: High Desert Inferno 113
Chapter 17: Investigation and Findings 131
Chapter 18: Yarnell Fire 139
Chapter 19: Saturday, June 29, 2013. 144
Chapter 20: Sunday, June 30, 2013 147

Resources. 166
About the Author 167

CHAPTER ONE

Entering the Season

Early spring is a beautiful time of the year. As the sun wends its way northward, winter grudgingly gives way to a fresh beginning.

Even before the last of the melting snow succumbs to the warming sun, new life begins to appear. Dark green spears of new grass push their way through the dead, matted grass of years past. A pair of impatient robins chirp excitedly as they choose the site for their new nest. As if by magic, the meadows become giant playgrounds as the new generation of frolicking wildlife are born. It is an exciting time.

In just a few short weeks, however, spring must yield to a more serious season—summer. It is a time that things must be done. Time to attend crops, to build, to complete tasks in preparation for the next cycle of seasons.

As the summer progresses, the heat begins to sap the moisture from the forests and grasslands. The life-giving rains of spring are scarce now. Preparations for a new battle with an old foe are about to begin.

In the past several years, drought has plagued the West. California's droughts are disastrous, with no relief in sight. The Northwest, Southwest, and intermountain West are not faring much better.

The wildfire season in 2020, in particular, was catastrophic for most of the western states, with over one hundred major fires. California,

Oregon, and Washington suffered immensely with dozens of fatalities and missing citizens. Whole communities and towns were burned to the ground. Over five million acres were destroyed throughout these states, setting new records for wildfires. California saw record-breaking temperatures with some areas around Los Angeles reaching 121 degrees Fahrenheit and Death Valley at 130 degrees Fahrenheit. Due to the ongoing drought and high temperatures, California could be battling wildfires year-round.

For more than a century, humans have sought to control and extinguish wildfires. Many of the most destructive fires were caused by carelessness.

Government agencies in charge of firefighting efforts begin planning for the wildfire season during the winter months, taking manpower, tools, equipment, and aircraft into consideration.

As the years have progressed, so have the means to battle wildfires. Airplanes, helicopters, satellites, infrared scanning devices, and improved weather predictions are just a few of the weapons now used to combat the flames. With all the modern equipment and technology available, quite often, it still is not enough to keep the fires at bay.

In early spring, the hiring and training of personnel begins. Many of these folks are returning seasonal employees, while others are new hires. Some will stand guard at the fire lookouts, while others will maintain trails and campgrounds and perform dozens of other tasks required to maintain our national forests, parks, and public lands. Most of these employees will be cross-trained for one other thing in common—wildland firefighting. Most, if called upon, will act in a supporting role to the professionals who are employed solely for firefighting purposes.

CHAPTER TWO

Tragedy on the Selway

Despite all the planning, training, and preparations, no one could possibly foretell the chain of disastrous events that would take place starting in early spring and ending in late summer of 1979. This was a year designed for tragedy.

The spring of 1979 started out normally. As in previous years, the snow melted in the high country and began to fill the reservoirs with water vital to the valleys for irrigating crops and orchards.

In late May and early June, abnormally hot weather began to dry out the lower country. As it continued, the higher elevations began to feel the effects of the heat.

At the little airstrip just outside of Grangeville, Idaho, the air was filled with the excited chatter of the ten passengers milling about the aircraft parking ramp. The US Forest Service employees would soon be boarding the twin-engine DC-3 that squatted smugly on the ramp. The thirty-five-year-old airplane had already established itself as legendary. Having evolved back in the 1930s, the DC-3, in the minds of many seasoned aviators, was the best and most reliable aircraft to ever take to the skies. The DC-3, also known as the "Doug," "Dakota," and for some unflattering reason, the "Gooney Bird," had created a reputation that is hard to surpass to this day.

DC-3 N146Z. Sister ship of N148Z. COURTESY OF GERARD HELMER.

The DC-3 has seen service in just about every country in the world. A veteran of World War II, the Burma Airlift, the Korean War, and the Berlin Airlift, the DC-3 was also used as a gunship in the Vietnam War, where it gained yet another nickname, "Puff the Magic Dragon."

This US Forest Service DC-3 had a good reason to look smug. Its primary purpose was to transport Forest Service smokejumpers into action. The smokejumpers, considered some of the most elite wildland firefighters, felt as safe in the Doug as they would in their own living rooms. Even seasoned jumpers who had parachuted from the vintage, reliable Ford Trimotors could not find much reason to fault the Doug.

On June 11, the DC-3 would be making a routine flight to a remote airstrip and Forest Service camp called Moose Creek. The camp, located in one of the most isolated and primitive areas in the lower forty-eight states, is used as a training camp for employees and as a base for patrolling the Selway-Bitterroot Wilderness area. The sixty-mile flight would take approximately thirty minutes. N148Z would never complete this short flight. Within an hour of departing Grangeville, the airplane would lie crumpled in the swift moving water of the Selway River.

The accident investigation report gives an explanation and purpose for this flight:

USFS DC-3 at Moose Creek landing strip.

ACCIDENT SITUATION

Annually, at the beginning of the field season, the Moose Creek Ranger District conducts a week-long wilderness management training session for new and returning employees. The Moose Creek District is almost totally wilderness with only 300 acres of the 560,000 acres not within the Selway-Bitterroot Wilderness. The District maintains an office in Grangeville year round, but moves the majority of the workforce and activity into backcountry with headquarters generally at Moose Creek Ranger Station at the junction of Moose Creek and the Selway River (within the Wilderness) for the summer. The wilderness training is conducted at Moose Creek Ranger Station.

On June 11, 1979, at about 08:30 PDT, Forest Service DC-3 148Z left McCall for Grangeville en route to Moose Creek Ranger Station. The pilot reported in on the Forest net radio when approximately 10 minutes out of Grangeville. After an apparently uneventful flight, 148Z landed at Grangeville and was loaded with approximately 3,102 pounds of cargo, seven District personnel who were to participate in the wilderness management training and then begin their field assignments, two Nezperce Forest engineering personnel who were to handle preliminary design of a new water system for the ranger station, one volunteer from the Red River Ranger District, the pilot and copilot, and two dogs.

The manifest listed the following passengers and crew:

Name	Title
Hagen, Ronald L.	Civil Engineer
Taylor, Robert A.	Civil Engineer Technician
Easthouse, Donald M.	Forester
Terkeurst, Thomas J.	Volunteer
McGreevey, Patrick J.	Forestry Aid
Dietz, Charles H.	Forestry Technician
Leber, Phillip K.	Forestry Technician
Hodgin, Catherine S.	Forestry Technician
Stringham, Bryant O.	Summer Aid
Cook, Robert B.	Forestry Aid
Hachmeister, Marvin B.	Pilot
Slingerland, John B.	Copilot

The interior of a DC-3 which is similar in configuration to N148Z. It shows the seating and cargo arrangement at the time of the crash. PHOTOGRAPH COURTESY OF THE US FOREST SERVICE.

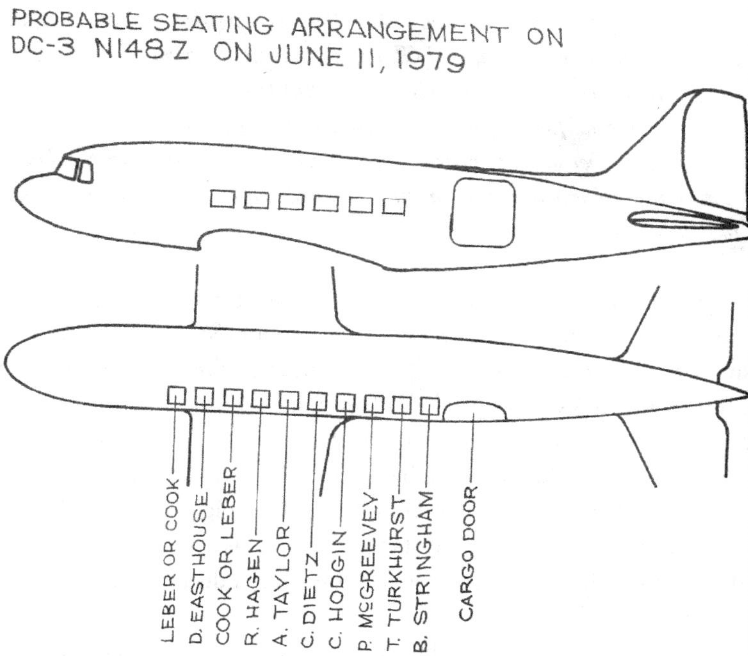

Probable seating arrangement on N148Z on June 11, 1979. DIAGRAM COURTESY OF THE US FOREST SERVICE.

The aircraft had been configured for smoke jumping and consequently, all of the passengers were sitting on the left side and facing the cargo on the right side.

The DC-3 148Z departed Grangeville at approximately 09:28 enroute to the airstrip at Moose Creek Ranger Station. The takeoff was apparently normal and at 09:30, the pilot reported takeoff using the Forest net radio. Two observers, one a private aircraft pilot, watched the aircraft take off and reported black smoke coming from the right engine for a short period during takeoff. The smoke stopped as the aircraft circled the airport. Both observers felt the smoke was not excessive or unusual, but rather the result of a "too-rich" fuel mixture.

A DC-3 aircraft, presumed to be 148Z, was sighted near the confluence of the Selway, Lochsa, and Clearwater Rivers by a commercial pilot. He felt the aircraft was approximately 2,000 feet lower in altitude than would be normal for the flight to Moose Creek, a flight he has made many times. He neither saw nor heard anything else unusual; however, this location is approximately 9 miles north of the normal route from Grangeville to Moose Creek.

For seventeen-year-old Bryant Stringham, it was to be the start of a summer job at the Moose Creek Ranger Station. Stringham patted his small dog tied next to his seat. The little beagle calmed as the soothing hand of his master scratched the floppy ears. Earlier, on the parking ramp, the dog had bristled at the sight of the much larger German shepherd being held on a leash by one of the other passengers.

After the training session, twenty-five-year-old Catherine Hodgin of Eugene, Oregon, would be starting her job as a fire tower lookout. The German shepherd would be her companion during the long summer vigil.

In the cockpit, Whitey Hachmeister and John Slingerland were busy scanning instruments and maps as they flew toward their destination, Moose Creek airstrip. Both men were retired military pilots. Whitey had flown transports for the US Air Force, while Slingerland had flown jets for the US Navy. Both men enjoyed flying for the Forest Service and the excitement that a summer of firefighting activities can bring.

As the DC-3 approached the rugged canyon of the Selway River, the port engine either quit or was shut down. The airplane began descending toward the canyon. The pilots would have increased the throttle on the starboard engine to maintain airspeed and altitude. Next, they would go through the procedure of feathering the windmilling propeller of the dead engine. Unbeknownst to the pilots, an unimaginable chain of events was about to take place when the power was increased on the right engine.

Inside the cabin, an eerie silence had fallen over the passengers. Bryant Stringham peered out the left side window and saw the motionless propeller of the dead engine and then, in his words, "The right engine blew up and caught fire." Bryant's ordeal was just beginning; his fight for survival was yet to come.

Far below, a group of hikers trudged their way along a wilderness trail. Their destination was also Moose Creek Ranger Station.

As the DC-3 rounded a bend in the canyon, the backpackers could see that the plane was in trouble. In eyewitness statements given to Forest Service investigators, Martin Hibbs of Spokane, Washington, noticed a plume of whitish vapor or smoke trailing under the right engine cowling. Immediately after, flames appeared from the engine cowling. John Herdrich, another member of the group, stated that the flames increased in intensity over the next ten seconds. Another hiker was Hal Blegen, a photographer for the *Spokesman-Review* newspaper in Spokane, Washington. As Blegen snapped pictures, the right engine, now fully engulfed in flames, suddenly fell away from the descending aircraft and plunged earthward, landing about a mile upriver from where the hikers stood in awe.

The witnesses stated that the aircraft appeared to stabilize and then disappeared from their sight. At the time, they thought the plane would make it to the Moose Creek airstrip.

The pilots struggled to maneuver the plane down through the canyon. With the left engine dead and the right engine gone, the DC-3 was nothing more than a glider, fighting for its life.

The only possible chance of survival would be to belly the airplane into the river. Just ahead at Dry Bar, a campground on the river, lay a fairly straight stretch of the river. Fearful of stalling if the airspeed dwindled too low, the pilots desperately attempted to extend the glide. The doomed airplane would go no further. The left wing smashed into a tree, ripping a fifteen-foot portion of the outer wing from the fuselage. The remainder of the plane plunged into the water.

The engine was trailing about 100 feet of flame until it got halfway to the ground and then the flame disappeared. PHOTOGRAPH COURTESY OF THE US FOREST SERVICE.

After the right engine had caught fire, Stringham estimates that the plane continued flying for another ten to fifteen minutes. The aircraft was low in the canyon by this time. "Nothing was said; it was real quiet. Everyone started buckling up their seatbelts," Stringham said. He recalls the moment of impact. "With a real big concussion, the plane

This is the tree that the left wing of N148Z struck just before impact. Note the mark a few feet below the point of fracture. The fracture occurred from whiplash after the impact. PHOTOGRAPH COURTESY OF THE US FOREST SERVICE.

smacked into the river and broke up on impact. I knew right away I wasn't hurt, but I was in a little bit of shock."

As the cold river water rushed in, the broken plane began to spin and started to sink. Stringham tried desperately to help the man next to him, attempting to hold his head above water, but to no avail. With his pocketknife, Stringham was able to cut the rope, freeing his struggling dog. As the broken fuselage swung around in the swift current, Stringham grabbed a floating sleeping bag and kicked his way out of the cabin. He was carried downstream and worked his way to several large rocks along the shoreline.

Upstream from where Bryant was, Robert Taylor, from Whitebird, Idaho, and Charles Dietz, from Republic, Kansas, had also survived the crash and gotten clear of the sinking plane. Taylor was severely injured and was in deep shock. They clung to a large rock surrounded by the rushing river.

Meanwhile, downriver, the party of backpackers began seeing sleeping bags, camping gear, and debris floating past them. They thought a river raft had overturned and dumped the gear into the river. Not until hours later when they came upon the wreckage did they realize that the airplane had not made it to Moose Creek.

When the DC-3 had not arrived within the proper time frame, a search and rescue plan was formulated within minutes. At the Missoula, Montana, smokejumper base approximately seventy air miles northeast of the crash site, a crew of jumpers were loading onto an airplane and were soon airborne en route to the crash site. Search aircraft were also launched from the Grangeville airport, currently known as Idaho County Airport. One of the search aircraft soon picked up a signal from an emergency locator transmitter, homed in on the beacon, and located the downed aircraft.

Stringham made his way back upriver, about 150 yards, to where the other two men were. After checking the condition of the other two survivors and rendering aid the best that he could, it was determined that Stringham should attempt to reach the ranger camp at Moose Creek

Wolf Creek Rapids, Selway River. PHOTOGRAPH COURTESY OF THE US FOREST SERVICE.

and seek help. Struggling up the rugged, almost impassable canyon and, by his own account, "two and a half miles out of some of the roughest country you'd ever want to see," Stringham came upon a packer leading a string of packhorses headed toward the crash site. Borrowing one of the horses, Stringham continued his journey toward the ranger station, finally breaking into the clearing at Moose Creek, arriving a little after 6:00 p.m. It was now over eight hours since he had left the airport at Grangeville on the ill-fated flight. After relaying the information of the crash, Stringham and his dog were airlifted to the Grangeville hospital.

Arriving over the crash site, the smokejumpers began parachuting into the treacherous canyon. Several of the smokejumpers were paramedics and began administering first aid upon reaching the two survivors. Taylor was in deep shock. The paramedics administered CPR in a desperate attempt to save his life. Approximately seven hours after the crash, Taylor succumbed to his injuries.

Other smokejumpers searched both banks of the swiftly moving river for other survivors. Miraculously, the German shepherd belonging to Catherine Hodgin had survived the crash. The dog had been swept downstream about two miles where it was found along the bank, shivering and in shock from a broken leg.

The main part of the aircraft's fuselage, with a portion of the right wing, had drifted downriver about two miles and become lodged against the rocks of the Wolf Creek rapids. A portion of the tail section was found farther downstream. Smokejumpers broke a hole into the tail wreckage but found only a helmet.

Because of the swift-moving water, recovery operations were hazardous. Divers flown in from Boise were in great peril during their search for victims. The force of the water crumpled and flattened the wreckage against the rocks.

Weeks would pass before all the victims would be found. The body of Whitey Hachmeister, the pilot, was the last to be recovered. After several delays due to weather and high water, a large helicopter finally lifted the remnants of the aircraft from the river.

CHAPTER THREE

The Accident Investigation

A team of highly qualified investigators were assembled almost immediately after the crash. All aspects of the crash were analyzed profusely.

Interviews with the two survivors, Bryant Stringham and Charles Dietz, were invaluable in determining the causes of this tragic accident. The fact that anyone even survived the crash was considered a miracle.

Bryant Stringham's interview was conducted by a team of four investigators. The interview was recorded and then later transcribed for the accident report. During the interview, it was not noted who each person was.

At times, there seems to be repetitive questions, but quite often it was to clarify previous discussions or answers to the questioning. During the interview, various maps, sketches, drawings, photographs, and hand gestures were used to determine the locations of the crash scene, the wreckage as it was swept downstream, and where the survivors were able to make it to shore.

The interview with Bryant Stringham by the accident investigators as recorded from the official accident report is titled DC-3 Aircrash Nezperce National Forest, Idaho, June 11, 1979.

THE FLIGHT AND THE CRASH

BRYANT: We left the airport after loading up, around 9:30. We took off, and as far as I could tell, everything was going right. About 5 to 10 minutes into the flight, the pilot went ahead and told us we could go up 1 or 2 at a time to look at the scenery and stuff. The guy who was sitting next to me and another guy up towards the front went on up there. Then about 15 minutes or so into the flight, I noticed the dog started acting like he was sick. He kept looking out the window, towards the right engine. Then a couple of minutes later, he wanted to get up on my lap and he kept looking back over his shoulder at where the right engine was. I let him up on my lap finally and let him look out the window there where I was sitting. He wouldn't look at the ground; he kept looking at the wing. He kept looking back over his shoulder where the right engine was all the time and then the left engine quit, and things got pretty quiet. He was running all over the place and I was trying to keep him under control. Then just right after that, flames started coming out of the engine. We just gradually lost altitude and hit the river. After a couple of vain attempts to help the guy next to me who had come back from the pilot's cabin and sat down, I got out of the craft. I just helped the other two who were down and injured.

INTERVIEWER: Bryant, have you ever flown in airplanes before or was this a first flight?

BRYANT: No, I have flown before. Last year, going to and from work. I flew I think six times last year.

INTERVIEWER: What kind of airplanes?

BRYANT: The first one I flew was a DC-3. We went in on that and this is the second time I have been on a DC-3. The rest were just little light aircraft that I flew out on after I reached Moose Creek.

INTERVIEWER: Now, when you got on this particular flight, where did you sit?

BRYANT: I sat on the seat, we were sitting on the left side of the plane on those seats that fold down, closest to the cargo doors.

INTERVIEWER: You said your dog was sitting on your lap and that he was nervous and looking out at the right engine.

BRYANT: Before he was seated right here on the corner of this seat and had his head looking at the cargo door because there was a breeze coming through there. (Author's note: From Bryant's description, his dog would have been sitting on the other side of the cargo doors toward the tail of the aircraft. The DC-3 was not pressurized; consequently, the cargo doors would allow a small amount of the airstream from the aircraft to filter a breeze inside.) He had his head into the breeze and about 5 minutes before the trouble began, he got really nervous, and he moved away from the cargo doors. He wanted to come clear up here to the front. He was tied down. He wanted to get on my lap and kept looking out this window here. He kept looking right in this area here. He'd tilt his head funny once in a while. I thought maybe he was just sick. He hadn't flown before.

INTERVIEWER: Did you look out to see what he was trying to look at?

BRYANT: Yeah, I was trying to follow his eyes and all I could see was this section of wing here and a little bit of the top. The other dog was really calm the whole time and did not do that. My dog kept looking funny and cocking his head. Once I got him on my lap and he would not look down at all. He only looked straight out there and over his shoulder.

INTERVIEWER: Had the dog ever been on an airplane before?

BRYANT: No.

INTERVIEWER: It was his first flight then.

BRYANT: Yeah.

INTERVIEWER: Now, if you think back and think about the first time you ever rode on a DC-3 and the noises that you heard and everything. Would you describe this flight?

BRYANT: I didn't notice any difference. It was just real loud in there. It sounded like he throttled down and the engine quit. That's what I thought had happened.

INTERVIEWER: Had you flown in a DC-3 before with the door off? Was the door off?

INTERVIEWER: The door was not off. It was on.

BRYANT: The only difference between this flight and the other flight is that I was seated on the right side instead of the left.

INTERVIEWER: Okay now, you said it sounded like he throttled back?

BRYANT: Yes. That is the impression I got. I thought we were getting fairly close to the station and when it got quiet, I thought he had just throttled back. But at that point, the dog was going nuts, and I was trying to keep him under control.

INTERVIEWER: Now, when it got quiet, can you describe that?

BRYANT: Yeah. I heard one engine going, but it wasn't long after that when flames began to come out and I watched the flames a while thinking it was only a reflection of the sun or something until I looked out the window and I seen the fire going along the sides.

INTERVIEWER: How long would you say that was between the time you heard the throttle back here?

BRYANT: I would say it was at most 30 seconds—it wasn't very long. It was just a really short time. It seemed like it was a long time, but I was sure that I remember it throttling back and the dog was trying to get under my arms and right after that the right engine started on fire.

INTERVIEWER: What did you see when you looked out the window at this engine?

BRYANT: I just seen a whole bunch of fire and smoke.

INTERVIEWER: Where was the fire? Top? Bottom? Sides?

BRYANT: It seemed like it was burning from up here somewhere and it was running clear back here along the side of the plane. It was getting really hot on the inside of the plane. You could feel the heat. (Author's note: The fire was streaming from the right engine, over the wing, and then pushed toward the metal fuselage, opposite of Bryant's location.)

INTERVIEWER: Could you tell whether the fuselage was going straight like that?

BRYANT: It was just going slightly down, just at a real slight angle and it kept at that angle clear until we hit that tree over there where we hit, and it seemed like it stayed at pretty much the same angle, but it just picked up speed.

INTERVIEWER: Would you say the fuselage was going straight through the air even though down like that?

BRYANT: Yeah. I would say so. It was bucking around but it was keeping pretty well straight, just slightly down all the time.

INTERVIEWER: You are saying the angle of descent was down like that but not like this?

BRYANT: If it would have been up like that then it would probably have been looking more level. It was pretty well level, but it was going about an angle with the nose. Just slightly down.

INTERVIEWER: I am interested as to where the flames hit.

INTERVIEWER: Could you maybe just make some, did it cover the whole top and side or just?

BRYANT: From the window that I seen, I just noticed the flames. I seen something like this (sounds of drawing on background of tape).

INTERVIEWER: The flames came in toward the fuselage by your drawings here?

BRYANT: Yeah, it seemed like they was brushing right along the windows there. They could have been out there further but that's how it seemed to me.

INTERVIEWER: They were extending back that way?

BRYANT: As far as I could see out this window. I looked back out this window before the guy came back and I noticed some smoke or something back there.

INTERVIEWER: There was another one of your buddies up here at the time in the cockpit?

BRYANT: Yeah, I think they were both up here and just shortly after the plane caught fire. He walked back and took his seat. The pilot was giving us orders on taking off our glasses, hold hands, and stuff. (Author's note: Charles Dietz, the other survivor, thought that one of the other passengers, Easthouse, might have been the one to issue these instructions.)

INTERVIEWER: Did he do that on the intercom?

BRYANT: Yeah.

INTERVIEWER: We'll go back and tie up a couple of points together that you made.

INTERVIEWER: One, you heard the engine noise, throttle back as you put it.

INTERVIEWER: Could you still hear another engine running?

BRYANT: Yeah, I heard the other engine.

INTERVIEWER: And at the time the throttle back occurred, we will try to sequence this with regard to throttle, the passenger that was up here in front with the pilot coming walking back, and the fire that was going. Which occurred first?

BRYANT: The throttle back, then the flames, then the passenger returning.

INTERVIEWER: This was the engine that was throttling back?

BRYANT: Yeah. That was the one that seemed to be. Because I looked out before we hit the ground, and I seen the prop and it wasn't turning. Right after this one caught fire, just shortly after that both engines were off. This one didn't stay running.

INTERVIEWER: When the first throttle back occurred did you look back at this engine or where did you look?

BRYANT: I didn't look out at any engine when the throttle back occurred. I looked out later, as we were going down further when this one was still on fire. Charlie told me later after the crash that he had seen the left engine quit.

INTERVIEWER: When did you first look at the left engine and see that it was not turning in relation to the fire?

BRYANT: Obviously, when we were nearly ready to crash.

INTERVIEWER: Is that right. It was some time then?

BRYANT: Yeah.

INTERVIEWER: When you looked at it, and you saw this propeller, what did it look like?

BRYANT: It looked like the air, we were going down, it was turning it real slow.

INTERVIEWER: Did you see the flat side of the prop itself?

BRYANT: I just seen it going around like that, it looked like just the air was pushing it.

INTERVIEWER: I am going to draw another picture here. From your position looking out the window, which one of these pictures resembles closely what you saw? (Author's note: The investigators were trying to determine whether the propeller had been feathered at this time when Bryant observed it.)

BRYANT: This one is probably the closest, because all I seen was just one blade at the time running.

INTERVIEWER: Well I put the wing right there.

BRYANT: Yeah, that one looks right.

INTERVIEWER: This one here. In other words you saw a thin blade rather than a big fat blade like that?

BRYANT: Yeah, it was a little bit more bulky. (Author's note: From Bryant's description, the propeller blades were most likely in the feathered position.)

INTERVIEWER: Bryant, going back on your first DC-3 ride that you talked about. You said this was your second one. Was that going into Moose Creek?

BRYANT: Yes.

INTERVIEWER: How would you compare the altitude that you were flying on this flight with the first time you flew out to Moose Creek on a DC-3?

BRYANT: It seemed like at first it was real comparable, we flew about the same. I liked to watch the ground when I fly and it was about the same.

INTERVIEWER: Could you estimate about how high you were? Are you any judge of distances above the ground?

BRYANT: I can't judge anything above ground. I don't have any ideas. I noticed that when we got into the canyon there that we were maybe level or slightly above the top of the mountains.

INTERVIEWER: You mean as you started up the Selway? Is that what you were referring to?

BRYANT: Yeah.

INTERVIEWER: This is before any trouble?

BRYANT: Yeah, just before.

INTERVIEWER: Now, you said that there was throttle back and there was noticeable fire. But you didn't tell me anything about the colors in the fire?

BRYANT: It was orange fire. I seen a lot of (it) reflected off the side. And what I saw from the windows was an orange color, like when you light a match or something.

INTERVIEWER: Did there seem to be a lot of smoke with the fire?

BRYANT: Yeah, it seemed like it was smoking a little bit and I thought it was burning the plane, but I guess it wasn't it was just burning the fuel.

INTERVIEWER: What was the situation inside the aircraft at the time the fire was going?

BRYANT: It was real quiet. Just watching the fire.

INTERVIEWER: I mean other than the people themselves?

BRYANT: The plane was just bucking real hard the whole time.

INTERVIEWER: Was there any smoke or fire or anything in the plane itself?

BRYANT: No, there wasn't anything got in I don't think. It was on the outside, I just noticed you could feel the heat from the fire.

INTERVIEWER: There was no smoke inside the plane, that you were aware of?

BRYANT: Not that I was aware of.

INTERVIEWER: Now Bryant after he lost this engine here, and this one was on fire, did you hear any bumping on the bottom side of the airplane? Any unusual noise on the bottom side?

BRYANT: No, the only noises I noticed was it sounded like there was someone out there shaking on the wing. A kind of grating flapping sound.

INTERVIEWER: Which wing?

BRYANT: It seemed like it was the right one.

INTERVIEWER: Now did you observe what was going on in the cockpit? Was the cockpit door open so that you could actually see where the pilots were?

BRYANT: You could if you would have leaned way out here. It was open I think, but the way that I was seated I couldn't see into it. But I seen that the doors were open.

INTERVIEWER: You were describing a while ago that you were descending and that the noise level was quiet. Would that be the way you described it?

BRYANT: Yeah it was real quiet without both the engines. Just real quiet. You could hear the flames. It sounded like something was shaking that wing, loose tin foil or something.

INTERVIEWER: Now, how long did you notice flames? Were there flames all the way down?

BRYANT: It seemed like there was, but it's really hard to tell now that I have seen pictures of it and it shows all the flames going with the engine itself when it fell off. It seemed to me like there was flames but I could have been wrong because I was scared at the time.

INTERVIEWER: Can you use your hand here as an airplane and describe for us from the (time) the trouble started all the way down until the aircraft actually landed?

BRYANT: It was flying along pretty level here and there was real little turbulence. After the trouble started, there wasn't any noticeable difference from the time the left engine quit and the right engine caught fire. Just shortly after the engine caught fire and it started bucking a lot, it seemed like it was getting throwed forward and all around a little bit. And then it started to gradually descend, it was going steadily down, but not at a real sharp angle. We followed the river. It seemed like we wasn't over the river when the fire started, but then it seemed like we took a real sharp turn like this to get over the river and then banked over and then we were over the river. All I could see of the river was the very little edge and the trail and then it was still going down and bucking a bit. The closer we got down the more it would buck. Right towards the end it was coming down like this and I remember hitting something and thinking it was a tree and then it picked up speed and went in an angle about like this.

INTERVIEWER: How about the wind condition. The noise at the door. Was there any change in the air passing by the fuselage? Any noticeable difference in that sound?

BRYANT: It seemed like we were going a lot faster just from the time we hit that tree. It just seemed like we just picked up a lot of speed all of a sudden. It seemed like we were going fairly slow until we hit that tree, and then it seemed like just really, really fast.

INTERVIEWER: Did the angle of descent seem to remain the same or increase?

BRYANT: It seemed to remain pretty much the same because I was constantly looking down at the other people and if it had increased too sharp, I would have been looking down at them instead of more level. It was just real slight, the whole time.

INTERVIEWER: Was there any pitching of the plane to one side or the other after what you considered to be the impact with the tree or did the plane seem to be in a level?

BRYANT: When it hit the tree, it kind of hit like this or maybe a little bit to the side like this.

INTERVIEWER: To the right a little like that?

BRYANT: Yeah, it seemed. I figured it was the left wing from the way it sounded and everything. It seemed kind of like it hit like that, but it straightened out again.

INTERVIEWER: In your estimation the plane struck the water in a fairly flat trajectory—that is not a trajectory but it was not pitched to one side or the other—it was more or less parallel, the wings were more or less parallel with the river surface?

BRYANT: Yeah, more or less it might have been (in a) slight incline.

AFTER CRASHING INTO THE RIVER

INTERVIEWER: Let's talk now that you landed in the water in the river and tell us what happened after that until the time you got out of the water itself.

BRYANT: First, I just sat there and then I looked up and I noticed that both cargo doors were open and by the way the pilot hollered back to open the hatches. I didn't know what the hatches were. I figured they were the cargo doors. He said it three distinct times before we went down and the last time, he actually screamed it out "Open the hatches." I fiddled with them a little bit, trying to get them open, but I didn't manage to slide them open but I noticed when we hit both doors were open. Water was already up to our lap by that time. When I was sitting there and looked up the water was already up to my lap. When I looked into the plane I seen 3 people and this side here was sheared away as much as I could see. I seen a piece of metal sheared this way and the cutting edge was out about neck level. Right above the guy that was sitting right by me there was a big flap down there—metal. He was leaning pretty near against that. I could not see any further than three feet. The whole bottom part of the plane from here back was completely intact. These here were still together, the two tail fins and the door sill.

INTERVIEWER: How about from your seat forward? How far forward could you see as far as the aircraft was concerned?

BRYANT: I could see about that much forward, about the first three seats.

INTERVIEWER: What was obscuring your view?

BRYANT: Metal.

INTERVIEWER: From the roof?

BRYANT: Yeah, it seemed from the side and roof together and there was a lot of water in there too.

INTERVIEWER: Was the nose at that time lower than where you were at? Was the nose more underwater than where your seat was? Was the plane fairly level?

BRYANT: The plane was fairly level in the water. When I got out of the plane though I kicked free of it after the plane had floated down quite a ways and right about here in the river in comparison. It was laying at an angle like this floating down the river this way.

INTERVIEWER: Backwards?

BRYANT: Yeah, it was floating not quite backwards. I was in the water right about here and I stopped swimming and I turned around and looked and from what I could see of it, the pilot's cabin was twisted at an angle.

INTERVIEWER: Here's the pilot's cabin up here. It was twisted up like this?

BRYANT: Yes. It was twisted up like that, sort of bended up.

INTERVIEWER: You are indicating that it was twisted up and over to the right.

BRYANT: It seemed like it was twisted a little bit to the right but mostly I noticed that it was kind of straight out. It wasn't to any side really bad, it was straight out of the water.

INTERVIEWER: Attached by the roof of the pilot's area yet? Attached along here?

BRYANT: Yeah. The roof and part of this side it seemed like. It was broken open right here and this area right through here was completely torn apart.

INTERVIEWER: By that you mean it was gone?

BRYANT: Well it was just ripped all over the place. And from here back, it was completely intact. I noticed one wing intact and I think it was this wing here. I didn't notice this wing when I got away from the plane at all. So this one might have been completely gone. When I got out of the river and I looked back at the plane again it was coming right towards me at an angle about like this. This was still intact until it hit the rocks along the side and it took all this off. I noticed the wing and I am pretty sure it was this wing here. I didn't notice any engine and I didn't notice this any more. This might have fallen off. I didn't notice it when it floated by me. That might have been gone too.

INTERVIEWER: Bryant, where do you figure that the aircraft landed in the water?

BRYANT: Right up here to the top and straight stretch in the last 3rd quadrant.

INTERVIEWER: The last third of the straight stretch?

BRYANT: Yeah, because we floated down quite a way. I am not sure how long it laid there. Then the plane went around the bend here. I stayed with the plane through all these here and I guess that drybar was right where we were at cross stream. So I got out of the river right about here.

INTERVIEWER: What do you mean you stayed with the plane? You mean you floated in the river?

BRYANT: Yeah. I hung on to the cargo door, to the railing along the top, right in the door itself, so I could see everything coming. I just floated down river with the plane through all this rough water here, and it was still pretty rough when I got out. But we were right across from this bar here, the two survivors were.

INTERVIEWER: Now you say that you drifted on about 150 yards further on down?

BRYANT: Yeah. 100 to 150. In this area here. There's a lot of rock. The water is all pretty rough from here on down.

INTERVIEWER: What side of the river did you get out on?

BRYANT: The side opposite from the trail. It was this I think.

INTERVIEWER: Did you see any of your fellow passengers after you got off the airplane?

BRYANT: After I got out the only two I seen was these, but I seen three in the aircraft itself.

INTERVIEWER: After you got on shore, did you continue to watch the aircraft?

BRYANT: Yeah. It was floating just behind me, and I had to jump over the tail section. It came right straight along the rocks where I was standing, and I had to jump the tail section. So it was real close to the bank there at one point.

INTERVIEWER: When you were in the cargo door, floating backwards down the river was your view down the river? Could you see the river coming?

BRYANT: I could see the river coming.

INTERVIEWER: Okay, you were on the downriver side, in the plane then. But the plane was actually sitting something like this going down river. With the cargo door on this side, the down river side?

BRYANT: Yeah.

INTERVIEWER: You mentioned that the aircraft tail bumped into the bank or something?

BRYANT: It did. It scraped over on the side.

INTERVIEWER: You were out of the aircraft at that time?

BRYANT: Yeah. I was on the bank watching it.

INTERVIEWER: But at this point, where you have drawn this on the map, you were still in the plane?

BRYANT: I stayed clear around this bend here and down into this rough water here. I don't remember another bend. The water was rough. I wasn't paying any attention to the land. But I remember there was a big sandbar opposite where I walked out. It might have been downriver about 150 yards.

INTERVIEWER: When the airplane hit the water. What kind of jolt did you get?

BRYANT: Real solid.

INTERVIEWER: How far forward did you go?

BRYANT: As far as my seat belt. I got thrown forward and I remember just stopping. I had my head down so I don't remember getting my head whipped around. I went down, and it seemed like I went forward and all the way around as far as my seat belt would let me go. Then when I came to resting I was sitting hunched over on the seat just like I was before we went down.

INTERVIEWER: Okay, then what was your first act after that?

BRYANT: I just sat up and looked around and noticed that the doors were open and I noticed the people and the water.

INTERVIEWER: What did you do to get out of that? Did you get out at that time?

BRYANT: No. I even stayed fastened in my seat belt, clear until we entered into the rapids here. We went around the point there and the bend and rapids started about here somewhere. Just before I went into the rapids then, I undid my seat belt.

INTERVIEWER: Before that you stayed in the cabin?

BRYANT: Yes. I was just sitting in the cabin.

INTERVIEWER: Were you holding your dog yet or did the dog get away?

BRYANT: Yeah. I held him clear up until seems like right down here there is a real smooth stretch in the river and I turned him loose and threw him out the door. I watched him swim off, but I was afraid to let go of the plane because it was flooding real good.

INTERVIEWER: After you got out and you made it over to the bank and you continued to watch the aircraft. What happened afterwards? How far down the river could you see the aircraft?

BRYANT: I was probably about here and I watched it go all the way down and it seemed like maybe it turned this way so maybe I was through here somewhere. It seemed like it washed all the way down until it made a turn. So this here might have been the turn.

INTERVIEWER: It went out of sight. You watched it go around the corner?

BRYANT: Yes. I just kept watching it.

INTERVIEWER: Did it stay pretty much together the way you had seen it initially?

BRYANT: Pretty much so. The only difference was I can't remember now, but I might have seen it then, but I can't remember seeing the pilot's cabin and one of the wings. I am pretty sure it was the left wing. Then the tail section had been ripped off, but that had been ripped off by the rocks in front of my feet.

The tail section of N148Z in the Selway River. This scene is downstream of the crash site, where the section had come to rest in slower water. PHOTOGRAPH COURTESY OF THE US FOREST SERVICE.

INTERVIEWER: Where you were standing?

BRYANT: Yes.

INTERVIEWER: You got out of the plane and got ahead of it and got to the shore before it caught up with you. Is that what you are saying?

BRYANT: Yeah. I got away from the plane and then I swam as fast as I could to get away from it. It looked in the water when I first got out like it was swinging around here real fast and I thought it was going to catch me. So I left the plane right about through here and it took me right along the bank, and the plane was right about here coming down. I just got on the bank when the plane came by.

INTERVIEWER: The thing really floated good?

BRYANT: Yeah. It seemed to float pretty good.

INTERVIEWER: It was pretty much intact.

BRYANT: Pretty much so, yes.

INTERVIEWER: All the way from back here and the tail section?

BRYANT: Yeah.

INTERVIEWER: Were the wings connected on to all that you were looking at?

BRYANT: I just noticed one wing. I seen one wing. It was intact pretty well. I seen about that much of it when it was floating down.

INTERVIEWER: Do you think this other part here was gone?

BRYANT: Well, it could have been. But I remember when I first got out of the water I seen the whole plane except for one wing.

INTERVIEWER: Even the front of the fuselage area?

BRYANT: Um-hum. I don't remember seeing it, but I could have and just don't remember it. I did see from here back was completely intact. I didn't even see that part at all.

INTERVIEWER: When you were sitting in your seat after the initial contact, if you looked up could you see the ceiling?

BRYANT: Yeah. The ceiling was in there.

INTERVIEWER: This little line here will represent the water level and you will be in the water looking back at the aircraft. You can probably turn this off, we are going to try to reconstruct this drawing. (Author's note: It is likely that investigative tools such as slide projectors, recorders, and video cameras, not in use at the time, were turned off while reconstructing the drawings on a chalk board.)

INTERVIEWER: Now, according to the drawing that we have drawn here, Bryant, it appears that the front cockpit section of the aircraft is torn and twisted and disintegrated and pushed up and twisted to the left somewhat, but still it is raised up and to the right and you were actually looking more or less at the top of the cockpit or the fuselage cockpit section. And looking at the rest of the ship at the cargo door. The water level being about estimating what halfway up on the ship or where would you guess?

BRYANT: I guess halfway up.

INTERVIEWER: You could not reach the top of the ship enough to get on top?

BRYANT: No. I could reach up to about here.

INTERVIEWER: You could reach 6 to 8 inches above the cargo door?

BRYANT: Yeah. I had the cargo rail and I could pull myself up.

INTERVIEWER: From where you were in the water?

BRYANT: Yeah.

INTERVIEWER: Did the water cover the windows on the side?

BRYANT: No. The windows were like that.

INTERVIEWER: Slightly submerged. Bottoms of them.

INTERVIEWER: By your drawing these windows in here at the water level, was this portion in front of your seat, from your seat towards the cockpit. Was that portion of that fuselage still intact?

BRYANT: Yes. Pretty well.

INTERVIEWER: Was it broken open?

BRYANT: No, it wasn't broken open. From the inside it looked like it was torn up really bad, but from the outside it didn't appear to be torn up. From the inside as I looked down.

INTERVIEWER: Just draw a circular view from the inside.

BRYANT: Water was up to here. The seats here. The water was up some places higher than others. There was a flap of metal torn down like this and it was really jagged right through here.

INTERVIEWER: What color was that metal?

BRYANT: Kind of a light steel. I wasn't sure what the inside was made of and I was thinking that maybe it was plastic or something. I figured it was metal when I looked at it. And it looked really jagged and sharp.

INTERVIEWER: Do you recall anybody saying anything?

BRYANT: It was real quiet and no one even when we hit the water and the girl or no one screamed. No one said a word. I never heard anyone say anything. Never heard a moan or anything after we hit.

INTERVIEWER: When you got out of the plane and were in the water, did it appear to you that the entire fuselage of the aircraft from stem to stern was still attached? That is, broken up but all the pieces were there from tail to the nose.

BRYANT: It seemed to be but I can't tell too much about this area here. Whether that was gone or what.

INTERVIEWER: Just behind the cockpit.

BRYANT: Yeah.

INTERVIEWER: But you are saying that there might have been a chunk taken out of this area, there may or may not have been a chunk taken out, but you could still see the nose?

BRYANT: Yeah.

INTERVIEWER: That's when you were outside?

BRYANT: Yes.

INTERVIEWER: So when you initially saw the plane when you were in the water it appeared that the plane perhaps minus a wing, all of it from stem to stern was attached somehow one part to another?

BRYANT: Um-hum.

INTERVIEWER: As you were looking out, you say that one part of the wing was gone, did you notice if the propeller was still out there?

BRYANT: I didn't notice. If it was the right wing, then I don't think the engine was there.

INTERVIEWER: What about the left?

BRYANT: I didn't notice the left wing at all. It seems as I looked back on the plane floating down the river that I seen the right wing, but I don't ever remember seeing this wing. As far as I know it was the right wing, not the left one.

INTERVIEWER: How long would you say you were in the water?

BRYANT: In the plane or out of the plane?

INTERVIEWER: In the water total?

BRYANT: It's hard to say. I would say quite a while. I floated quite a ways.

INTERVIEWER: In the plane? You mean with the plane?

BRYANT: Both in and out of the plane. I was in the water quite a while, probably at least three minutes. I don't know how long it took me to swim, but it took me quite a while to swim from right through here somewhere. It took me quite a while it seemed to go from there to there, but I had been in the plane in the water to at least there. I stayed with the plane all the way through the rougher parts of the water here and I dove in about here.

INTERVIEWER: That's about a mile, right? From here to here. Maybe three-quarters.

BRYANT: Where's the bridge at?

INTERVIEWER: It's got to be up in here someplace. You hit here and you got out down here. That's where you separated yourself?

BRYANT: Yeah, I separated myself right through here somewhere.

INTERVIEWER: After the first rapids?

BRYANT: Yeah. I know I walked back about 2 miles through all this to the bridge, and from them 2 miles, it was about 150 yards beyond that. So if you clock it from the bridge to where I wrecked it was just slightly over 2 miles.

INTERVIEWER: Bryant, do you know what this portion of the wing is here?

BRYANT: It's the flaps.

INTERVIEWER: Whenever you were descending did you see what position that was in?

BRYANT: I noticed them at the time I noticed, the flaps, one of them seemed to be working, but I can't really remember though.

INTERVIEWER: Do you have any recollection of the gear going down?

BRYANT: I couldn't have seen that.

INTERVIEWER: You didn't hear anything?

BRYANT: I didn't hear anything.

INTERVIEWER: Are you referring to lowering the landing gear? Is that what you are saying?

BRYANT: Um-hum.

INTERVIEWER: I only have one more question I would like to ask. I would like to go back and cover one more time while you were flying just prior to the problem starting with the engines, and go through it one more time, as to the sequence as to how it occurred.

BRYANT: Okay. There was two people up in the cabin. And just before all this trouble happened, I thought the engine idled down.

INTERVIEWER: The left engine?

BRYANT: Yeah, the left engine. And shortly after that, the right engine caught fire and a little while after that the guy walked back and sat down.

INTERVIEWER: The guy who? One of the passengers. Right?

BRYANT: Yeah. From the description I was able to give to the secretary in Grangeville, she thinks it was the volunteer.

INTERVIEWER: You say he walked back and sat down. How far from you was he sitting?

BRYANT: Right in the next seat. Like when we were holding hands, my hand was right about there. So he was real close.

INTERVIEWER: Was anything said?

BRYANT: Yeah. He came down and sat down and buckled up his belt and me and the guy here had been holding hands and then he came down and sat down here and he buckled up and he was just sitting here like this and I told him that we were supposed to hold hands and he held his hands out and they were shaking real bad and I just grabbed it and held it real tight and that was all that was said until the pilot started saying open the hatches and that was just a little ways before we went down.

INTERVIEWER: Okay. I have no more questions. Roy? Bob? Jim?

INTERVIEWER: No.

This concluded the interview with Bryant.

CHAPTER FOUR

The Engines Investigation

A team of investigators was assigned the task of looking into the history and teardown of the aircraft's engines. Recovery of the engines from the swift, cold river would prove to be an arduous task. By running a cable from riverbank to riverbank, divers and recovery personnel were able to tie a raft to the cable and then maneuver the raft into position over each engine.

To help the reader understand the complexity of what the investigators had to confront during the two engines' teardown and inspection, a brief introduction and history of the type of engines that were installed on the crashed DC-3 is explained.

The engines were manufactured by the Pratt & Whitney Company. The engines were designated as R-1830-92, a high-octane, gas-fueled radial engine. Each engine was equipped with fourteen cylinders (two rows of seven cylinders) in a circular design. Each engine produced 1200 horsepower.

The investigators would be faced with several critical factors. First, they would have to determine what damage had occurred due to the crash, and in the case of the right engine, why it fell from the aircraft.

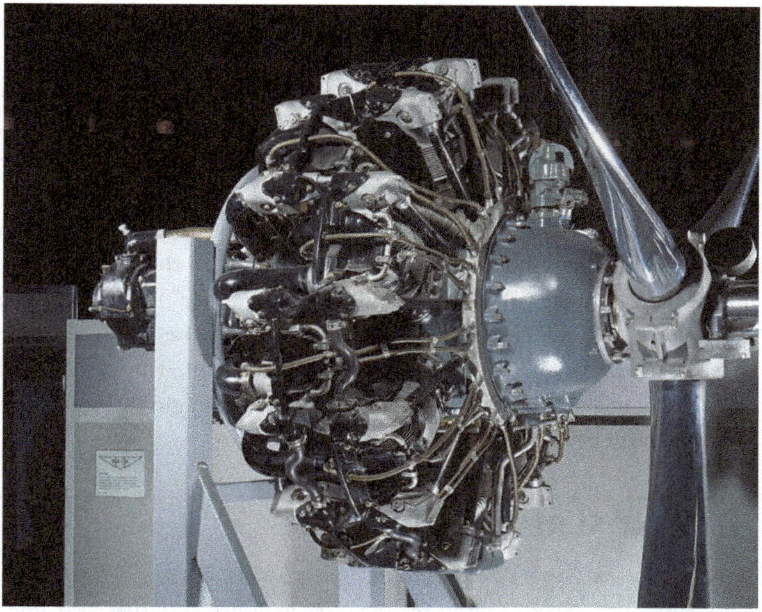

Pratt & Whitney R-1830-92. PHOTOGRAPH COURTESY OF SMITHSONIAN AIR AND SPACE MUSEUM.

Second, they would need to determine the condition and operating performance of each engine prior to the crash. This would be a task that would require a forensic-like investigation.

At times, parts of the investigation will seem trivial and a waste of time, such as the scrutiny of the cylinder washers that were a mixture, made up of different metals. However, as the reader will discover, this apparently innocent mistake would ultimately prove a major determining factor in the crash. Often, the engine investigations can seem overly tedious, but the results they yield are necessary to pinpoint the contributing causes of an accident.

On June 21, both engines were retrieved from the Selway River. A helicopter with an external cable attached to the belly hook lifted each engine from the river; the right engine was the first to be recovered.

Prior to lifting the left engine, it was confirmed that the propeller was indeed in the feathered position.

Upon recovery, the engines were taken to the Grangeville airport where they were then loaded onto a Forest Service DC-3. On June 22, the engines were transported to and offloaded at Steward-Davis overhaul facility located at Long Beach Airport in California.

Steward-Davis aircraft engine specialists would begin the thorough teardown and analysis of both engines as reported in the "Disassembly Report and Damage Analysis for US Forest Service" included in the official DC-3 accident report. Representatives from the US Forest Service, Federal Aviation Administration, and Morrison-Knudsen would participate in the teardown and observation of the engines. They began with the left engine.

ENGINE SERIAL NUMBER 142062

The left engine, Serial No. 142062, was overhauled during 1975 by Cooper Airmotive. Subsequently, the complete propeller reduction gear and housing assembly was removed, apparently to replace a defective unit on an operating aircraft. In 1977 another propeller reduction gear and housing assembly was installed on this engine by another contractor to the Forest Service.

Engine 142062 was installed on the subject aircraft during 1979, tested and accepted for flight, and operated a total of 15.7 hours before the crash landing.

As the dismantling commenced, the findings were recorded and photographed. The investigation report concerning the left engine states in part: "Nothing significant was noted until the front section (nose) of the engine was removed. The crankshaft to propeller shaft oil transfer pipe was found to be missing."

The report continues to describe the part number of the tube and other information concerning the propeller shaft rear bearing. The

Damaged left engine (left). Nose section showing oil transfer hole for missing 8-inch tube (right). PHOTOGRAPHS BY STEWARD-DAVIS INC., COURTESY OF THE US FOREST SERVICE.

report continues: "The supercharger section was disassembled. During disassembly, the main oil pressure relief valve body, part number 74663, was found to be loose. When the rear case was removed, a quarter-inch, metal, self-locking nut was found at the bottom of the intermediate rear case. This type of nut is not normally used in Pratt & Whitney engines of this type."

The significance of the missing oil transfer tube is covered and described by the engine teardown crew:

INTERPRETATION OF FINDINGS ON ENGINE 142062

Of the conditions noted during disassembly of the engine, none would result in performance symptoms or instrument readings to suggest the desirability of an engine shut down except for the missing oil transfer tube, part no. 36702, which is shown below and in front of the R1830-94 engine nose section in photograph #3.

This tube serves to transfer oil from the front end of the crankshaft to the interior of the propeller shaft. Oil supplied through this tube lubricates the propeller reduction gears and pinion gear bearings and, via the propeller distributor valve, applies pressure to the propeller pitch actuating piston so as to reduce pitch and increase RPM. Absence of this tube would have little or no effect on propeller feathering or unfeathering, it could only make the propeller slow to increase RPM.

Inquiries have been made of others who might have experience with R1830 engines in which the oil transfer tube was omitted, but no one has been found who can say with certainty what the exact effects or performance symptoms would be. Therefore, we must hypothesize on the effects and endeavor to reconstruct how absence of this tube in the subject engine could have resulted in its acceptance for flight and operation, satisfactorily for 15 hours before the crew of the ill-fated aircraft shut it down.

Nose section, left engine. A new oil transfer pipe was installed to show what it looks like. The original oil transfer pipe was missing. PHOTOGRAPH COURTESY OF THE US FOREST SERVICE.

The report describes how, even without the tube, some oil would still be able to transfer through the opening where the tube should be. Continuing with the likely chain of events concerning the left engine:

> *It is believed that an engine with the subject oil transfer tube omitted could be flight-tested and accepted for service after installation on an aircraft IF:*
>
> 1. *The engine was equipped with a high capacity oil pump with minimum internal clearances.*
>
> *Engine 142062 was so equipped and the pump had a new main body with almost zero clearance between the pressure pump element gears and the body.*
>
> 2. *The internal fits and clearances of parts of the engine were at the minimums so that oil flow through those parts would be at minimum. This minimum oil flow through the engine in all other areas would conceal the abnormal flow of oil leaking from the area flooded because of the missing transfer tube and the engine would still be able to maintain the required oil pressure during acceptance ground runs and test flights.*
>
> *We do not know if engine 142062 meets these criteria. Only reassembly and test with the pipe omitted could confirm this hypothesis.*
>
> 3. *The oil temperature throughout the acceptance tests remained below that which developed just before the engine was shut down.*
>
> *Again, only reassembly and test of the engine could define the critical oil temperatures.*
>
> *To continue this line of reasoning, it is believed that an engine with the transfer tube omitted and otherwise fitting the above conditions would be susceptible to a chain reaction of symptoms which could cause a pilot to perceive a cycle of rising oil temperature and dropping oil pressure which he would interpret as an incipient master rod bearing failure.*

This "chain reaction" would evolve as follows:

1. *Assuming the aircraft was more heavily loaded on its final mission than on previous flights with the subject engine, the flight would proceed at higher powers and lower air speeds than previously.*
2. *Engine temperatures and oil temperature would be higher than previously.*
3. *The higher oil temperature, the lower the oil viscosity and the thinner oil would leak more freely from the compartment containing the oil normally contained by the transfer tube. About 30% of the total leakage would be through the rings of splines, and 70% would flow forward, through the propeller tail shaft bearing, then thru the reduction drive gear bearing and then flooding the propeller reduction driving gear face where it meshes with the reduction drive pinion gears.*

As this flow would increase, the tail shaft bearing and reduction gearing, normally lubricated by a very light flow or mist of oil, would be increasingly loaded by the flood of oil and would generate a great amount of heat. As leakage increased, area E would be very heavily and uniformly flooded by the centrifugally distributed oil, generating extreme pressure and heat on the complete reduction gear train. Heat discoloration was noted on the reduction gear support bearings and on the inner tips of the fixed reduction gear teeth during disassembly.

Now the chain reaction once set off would proceed with the following sequence:

1. *Increased oil leakage.*
2. *Increased heat and thinning of the oil. (The pilot sees rising oil temperature.)*
3. *Increased oil flow into the propeller reduction gearing. (The pilot sees dropping main oil pressure.)*
4. *Increased oil leakage.*

5. *And so on ... until high oil temperature and low oil pressure cause the pilot to feel compelled to shut down the engine, believing he has the classic symptoms of a master rod bearing failure.*

It is also possible that as oil pressure dropped, the propeller would be slow to increase RPM which could suggest to the pilot that metal contamination from a failure was beginning to contaminate the propeller and governor.

The pace at which this situation could develop is unknown. Reassembly of the subject engine without the transfer tube and testing for the exact symptoms seems the only means of verification.

The preceding interpretation can account for the facts that:

1. *The subject engine was installed, tested, flown, and accepted for service. This means all instrument readings were found within limits and, the propeller feathered, unfeathered, and checked out normally.*
2. *The engine performed normally during the initial period of the ill fated flight.*
3. *The pilot, during this flight, perceived indications that caused him to shut down the engine—an engine which was found to have no failed or malfunctioning components, an engine in which the only discrepancy was the lack of a transfer tube, Part No. 36702.*

CHAPTER FIVE

Engine Serial Number 141621

Investigation into and the teardown of the right engine proved to be an even more bizarre and borderline sinister inquiry of the engines.

At the time of the investigation, the origin of the right engine was unknown. Investigators determined that the engine was overhauled with a total time of 8,000 hours. It was overhauled to zero hours by Gary Aircraft Corporation on February 6, 1973. The engine was installed on 148Z at an airframe time of 11,340 hours and 25 minutes by Morrison-Knudsen Aviation Center.

On September 19, 1978, a 100-hour inspection was performed on the airframe and right engine only. The time on the right engine had reached 1,049.0 hours. The 100-hour inspection on the left engine had been deferred since it was scheduled to be replaced.

On May 30, 1979, the preseason (fire season) inspection was completed by Morrison-Knudsen, again on the airframe and right engine only. The engine time was now 1,069.6 hours. The DC-3 had an estimated additional 8.5 hours of flight time from May 30, 1979, until the time of the crash on June 11, 1979. The total time on the right engine was 1,078.1 hours.

According to an entry in 148Z's logbook, the left engine was replaced by Morrison-Knudsen beginning on May 15 and completed on May 25, 1979.

The teardown report on the right engine continues:

Before disassembly of engine 141621, the following details were noted:

1. *The #8 cylinder, piston, and piston pin were missing from the engine. Only the bottom of the cylinder barrel from immediately above the mounting flange remained attached to the crankcase.*
2. *The #8 link rod was intact but damaged from flailing in the crankcase while the crankshaft was rotating.*
3. *There was no sign of the #8 piston pin which would have had to slip out of the #8 link rod rather than tear out, since the rod was unbroken.*
4. *Referring to Figure 2 and Photo No. 11:*
    a. *Cylinder hold down studs 15, 16, and 1 were found broken, and the nuts with stud remains were missing.*
    b. *On both sides of these three broken studs, the hold down nuts were loose or missing. Going clockwise from broken stud #1, #2 had a loose hold down nut and missing locknut and #3 was secure.*

Going counterclockwise from broken stud #15, #14 stud had no hold down nut, #13 was missing its lock nut and the hold down nut was loose by approximately 4 turns. #12 stud was broken with the nut and a stud remains missing. #11 nut was secure. Stud #8 was missing its lock nut but it is believed this was sheared off by impact from the cylinder barrel which can be seen to have come down with great force on studs 7 and 6, shown in Photo 11 bent outward and pulled from the crankcase.

Thus from broken stud #12 around to stud #2 with its loose nut, 7 studs are either broken or the nuts are loose or missing.

From stud #3 to #11 the 9 studs and nuts are secure or were damaged immediately before separation of the cylinder from the engine.

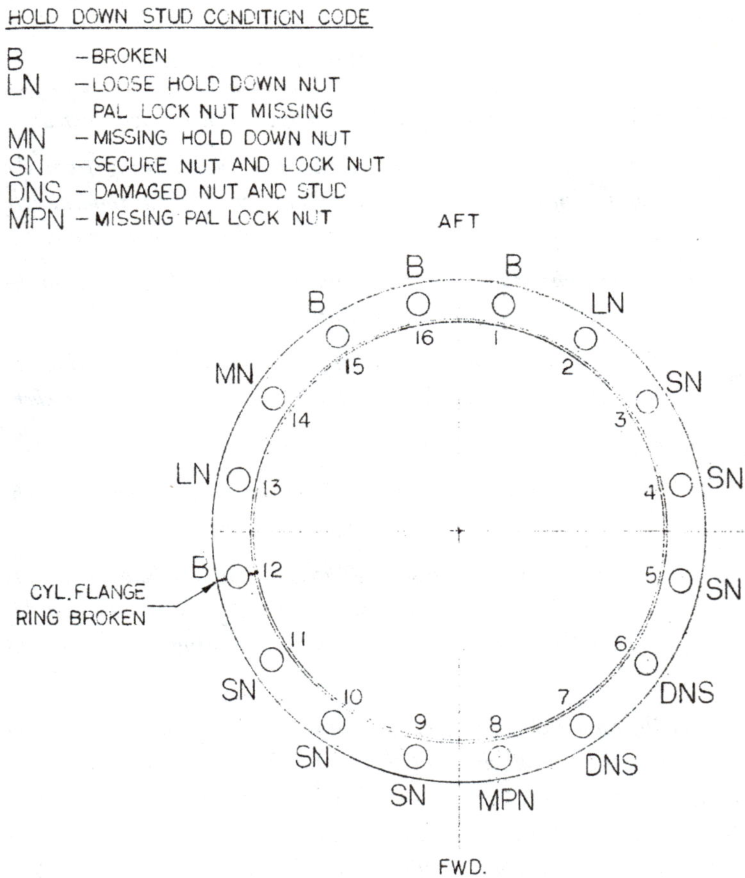

Number 8 cylinder flange and hold down studs. DIAGRAM BY STEWARD-DAVIS INC., COURTESY OF THE US FOREST SERVICE.

Cracked and damaged #8 cylinder flange of right engine. PHOTOGRAPH BY STEWARD-DAVIS INC., COURTESY OF THE US FOREST SERVICE.

The pre-teardown observation continues to describe other discrepancies and damage found due to the fire and impact of the engine falling from the plane into the river.

During the teardown and disassembly of the right engine, some shocking discoveries were made. We continue the report:

Following are the discrepancies noted:

1. *Two to three cylinder hold down nuts were found to be loose on each cylinder. Approximately half the cylinder base nut washers were bronze, part no. 31434, instead of the recommended superseding steel washers, part no. 110518, which have been recommended by Pratt & Whitney since April 22, 1946, per Service Bulletin No.*

> *706. The bronze washers were mixed indiscriminately with the steel washers on the No. 8 cylinder flange and on other cylinders, though several were noted to have 100% bronze washers.*
>
> 2. *Only the base flange portion of #8 cylinder remained on the engine. When it was removed, an entire section of the crankcase and cylinder hold down pad came free, extending from stud #5 to #12.*
> 3. *The #8 piston and piston pin were also missing.*
> 4. *The main oil pressure relief valve body, Part No. 74663, was only finger tight.*

The investigation into the right engine concludes with the investigators' and engine experts' findings.

> **INTERPRETATION OF FINDINGS ON ENGINE 141621:**
>
> *None of the conditions noted before, during, and after disassembly of the subject engine and its powerplant components would contribute to the failure of No. 8 cylinder, the fire in the powerplant or the subsequent detachment of the cylinder from the aircraft except the intermixing on individual cylinders of the bronze, P/N 31434, and steel, P/N 110518, cylinder hold down nut washers.*
>
> *The bronze washers were abandoned for use on higher powered engines such as the 1830-94 and R2000 models because they tended to cold flow slightly during service resulting in loss of tension and uniformity of tension on the cylinder hold down studs.*
>
> *Mixing steel washers with bronze washers indiscriminately on each cylinder could cause a situation in which:*
>
> 1. *The 16 studs which hold a cylinder down on the crankcase equally share the load when the cylinder is first installed and all of the hold*

down nuts are carefully torqued, tensioning each stud uniformly to, let us say, a load of 1000 lbs each.

2. *Under such an initial load, and subsequent operational loads, the bronze washers could cold flow into small spaces or imperfections in the cylinder flange and relieve the load on the affected stud. If the adjacent studs on each side of the bronze washer are fitted with steel washers, they must now share all loads previously taken by the stud with the bronze washer.*
3. *If, for example, four adjacent studs have bronze washers, and the next studs on each side of the four should have steel washers, then cold flowing of the bronze washers could transfer the loads from 2 studs onto each single adjacent stud.*

With various combinations of bronze and steel washers, the combinations of unequal loading of cylinder flanges and hold down studs grow rapidly and it should be noted that:

1. *Loosening of one cylinder hold down nut or stretching of one stud sets in motion a chain reaction potential in which the adjacent studs are overloaded and ready to yield at the first operational load, and upon their yielding, the next adjacent studs are more heavily overloaded and subject to early yielding which overloads the next adjacent studs, etc., etc., and finally to cylinder or crankcase failure.*
2. *An imperfection in a cylinder flange can be induced into a crack by unequal hold down stud tension and will further contribute to rapid multiplication of loads on adjacent studs with accelerated propagation of the crack.*

At the time of this writing, the metallurgical analysis of the No. 8 cylinder flange for the probable focus and evolution of the crack which resulted in its falling from the engine has not yet been received.

Subject to the findings of the metallurgical analysis, it would appear that the cylinder failure could have evolved as follows:

Assuming studs 13, 14 and 2 had bronze washers which flowed and relieved or the #13, 14, & 2 hold down nuts became a bit loose, a good portion of their load would shift onto studs 15, 16, and 1 as well as onto stud #12.

These studs and the cylinder flange would now be carrying a substantially increased load, resulting in propagation of the crack which is visible in photo 11 in the inner surface of the cylinder extending from between studs 15 and 1 to stud 12 where the crack moved vertically into the flange then radiated counter clockwise in the direction where all studs were still under full operational tension loads as compared with the opposite side of the cylinder where the stretched, relieved, or broken studs, and the original cylinder barrel fracture could no longer receive the operational loads.

On this hypothesis the crack would move around counter clockwise until it finally detached completely, during which a severe, tilted load would be applied to the crankcase so as to break loose the section referred to as illustrated in Photo #14.

At this point, it would have lifted with great force against the cowling & broken the cowling attach latches. This may have allowed the cowling to balloon somewhat at the bottom joint.

The cylinder barrel was probably bent so the piston could not pull out of it; therefore as the connecting rod pulled down into the crankcase it pulled the piston and the jammed cylinder down, out of alignment, so that the forward part of the barrel hooked over the cylinder portion still attached by the crankcase and drove studs 6 and 7 outwards as shown in Photo 11.

At this point, the piston would be pulled down against the edge of the remainder of the cylinder and would break up, leaving the piston pin in the link rod but the cylinder and piston free to break loose and fall through the gap in the cowling. Apparently at this point the piston pin somehow came free of the link rod without tearing the rod strap. The development of the fire and final detachment of the engine from the aircraft could then have progressed along the following lines:

With the cylinder beaten free of the engine which, despite the violence of the preceding events, the pilot had no choice but to keep operating since his other engine was shut down and presumed to be a failure, a combustible fuel mixture would now be spewing from the intake pipe and oil would be flowing heavily out of the open #8 cylinder position.

The oil would flow back, leak through the fire seal, and coat the interior of the accessory section.

Some of the fuel from the #8 intake pipe would probably condense and leak back over the cylinders, exhaust collector and into the accessory section. Some of the vaporized fuel (a perfect combustible mixture) would also flow back over the exhaust collector and into the accessory section.

With the engine being operated at full throttle as the pilot tried to hold altitude (the ballooned cowling would greatly increase the drag), the hot exhaust collector ring would inevitably finally ignite either the combustible mixture or the condensed fuel. It is clear that the flame moved forward to ignite the fuel coming from #8 intake pipe and that a hot, torching flame applied substantial heat to cylinders 7 and 9, melting head fins, baffles, etc.

The flame then moved into the accessory section, probably through the aforementioned engine accessory case drain line opening in the fire seal and connecting to the back of the oil sump immediately behind cylinder #8.

If a significant amount of condensed or vaporized fuel collected in the accessory section, then the passage of flame into the accessory section could have resulted in an explosive combustion.

In any event, by this time there was enough fuel, and oil in the accessory section to support enough of a fire to combine its heat with the vibration of the crippled, laboring engine, the oscillating cowling, and the violence of the cylinder failure to cause the engine to detach itself and fall free of the aircraft.

Conclusion

What should have been a short and scenic routine flight, beginning a season of training and employment for the passengers and crew on board the DC-3, turned into an unimaginable tragedy.

No one could foretell the chain of events that would cause this tragic loss of life. A small eight-inch tube missing from the left engine would not have caused this accident in itself, but combined with the other seemingly harmless mistakes (the removal of the engine fire extinguishers for routine maintenance and failure to reinstall them prior to releasing the aircraft for flight, and the installation of the wrong washers during an engine overhaul), it set the stage for this horrible accident. The wildfire season was off to a sad and tragic beginning.

The crash of N148Z was the second-worst airplane accident to take place in Idaho, surpassed only by the crash of a US Air Force C-123 East of Payette, Idaho, in October of 1958. The plane was carrying support members of the Air Force's famed Thunderbirds precision flying team and claimed the lives of nineteen crew members and passengers.

CHAPTER SIX

Cook Creek Ridge

The Boise National Forest (BNF) is located in west-central Idaho. It consists of 2.6 million acres and extends from Mountain Home, Idaho, in the south, to Yellow Pine, Idaho, 120 miles north. The BNF stretches approximately sixty miles east to west. To the delight of thousands of Idahoans and tourists, some of the most beautiful and rugged scenery in North America can be found within and adjacent to the forest. The eastern border of the BNF touches the famous River of No Return, the Middle Fork of the Salmon River.

As the search and recovery efforts for the missing passengers and crew of the DC-3 continued on the Selway, two hundred miles south of the crash site the hot temperatures and lack of moisture were preparing the battleground for the next contest against nature. Another challenge with a questionable outcome, yet to be determined.

On June 26, 1979, several bands of thunderstorms began moving into Idaho from the southwest. One particular storm drifted into Idaho from the vicinity of Ontario, Oregon, and moved slowly east–northeast. The storm rumbled ominously as it crossed Squaw Butte, a 5,896-foot prominent mountain just north of Emmett, Idaho.

The sun had been down for an hour, and the darkening sky was periodically lit by the bright whitish-orange flashes of cloud-to-cloud lightning. As if on cue, the huge frightening black mass suddenly erupted into a belching monster, spewing air-to-ground lightning. As large bolts careened toward the earth, each would suddenly splinter into silvery fingers of brilliant electricity.

The massive storm cell was being closely monitored by lookouts stationed on Scott and Whitehawk mountains. The people working the fire lookouts were attempting to record and keep track of the numerous and increasing lightning strikes. In the early morning, they would be searching these areas for smoke or fire starts.

Thirty-five air miles north of Boise, Idaho, at Garden Valley, the helitack crew was also watching the storm as it moved just north of the base. The helicopter attack crew is a group of highly trained firefighters who utilize helicopters for a fast and initial attack on newly started fires, especially fires in rugged, inaccessible mountainous terrain. Anticipating what the storm might produce, Ray Patnaude, the helitack foreman, notified the crew and pilot that they would be on duty at first light. Patnaude, a sixteen-year veteran of wildland firefighting and helicopter operations, knew what to expect from past experiences.

At 04:30 the following morning, the crew anxiously awaited what surely would be a busy day. Fire reports were being radioed into the dispatch center in Boise where they would then be evaluated and the necessary actions taken. The action could be dispatching smokejumpers, tanker planes, helitack, or all available resources, depending on the severity of the fire.

The first flight for the helicopter was a fire north of Garden Valley, Idaho, that had started from a lightning strike during the night. Several firefighters had hiked to the fire from a road two miles away.

The helicopter made several trips from Garden Valley with external sling loads, delivering water and other firefighting equipment. The chopper was then diverted to a location thirty miles southeast to retrieve some smokejumpers who had jumped on a fire the previous day.

Returning to Garden Valley and refueling, the helicopter was dispatched to a fire located thirty-six miles northeast of the helibase. Ray

Patnaude, Jeff Shinrock, Ron Taylor, and pilot Buz Sisk were airborne at 12:30, and approximately twenty minutes later, they were on scene. The helicopter orbited while Patnaude evaluated the situation and behavior of the fire. It was about one-half acre to three-quarter acres in size and growing, in heavy timber with some trees already beginning to crown out. He relayed the information to the forest dispatchers in Boise. He also suggested that more firefighters be dispatched to the fire. It was also relayed that there were old logging roads in the area and that pumper trucks and crew vehicles could get close to the active fire.

The helicopter landed on the logging road, and Shinrock and Taylor quickly unloaded their packs and equipment. Lifting off, the helicopter circled the fire, ensuring that the ground crew had radio communications. Directed to fly to the Lowman Ranger Station, the helicopter headed south for the ten-minute flight to the station.

Several more lightning-started fires were covered using firefighters from the Lowman District. Most of the fires were small, and usually two crewmen on each fire was enough to control and extinguish the blaze, provided it had been detected early enough.

Early the following morning, June 28, the helitack crew (minus Shinrock and Taylor) were again on standby. "Sleepers" were their main concern now. A sleeper is a potentially dangerous lightning-started fire that smolders and emits very little smoke. As the sun rises, warming the air, the winds begin to pick up, and the sleepers suddenly come alive.

As the morning wore on, the lookouts were not reporting any new smokes. The crew decided to grab lunch and began to relax, somewhat. At 12:10, the Boise dispatcher radioed the helitack base and told them to respond to a reported fire fifteen miles southwest of Garden Valley. Checking the map coordinates, the crew found that the fire would be close to Idaho State Highway 55, a road that followed the Payette River through a rugged canyon with steep slopes.

Helicopter H-10, the call sign of the fire attack helicopter, was airborne within four minutes after receiving the dispatch. The crew this time consisted of Patnaude, Dane Lee, Stan Kolby, and Sisk as pilot.

Photo of helicopter H-10. PHOTOGRAPH BY CHUCK KNEYSE, COURTESY OF IDAHO STATESMAN, 1979.

The fire had started along the highway when a wheel came off a boat trailer being towed by a motorhome. A shower of sparks spewing from the dragging axle torched off the tinder-dry grass and brush on the upslope side of the road. The wind, funneling up the narrow, rugged canyon, pushed the fire rapidly uphill toward heavy timber.

An Idaho state fire truck had just arrived and began spraying water on the south flank of the fire. Patnaude radioed the pertinent information to the Boise dispatch center. The fire was on Idaho state land and under Idaho state forestry jurisdiction, but under the mutual agreement, the US Forest Service could aid the state firefighters. It was decided that the helitack crew would be dropped off on a finger ridge about a quarter mile above the fire. H-10 made a low-level pass over a flat spot on the ridge. Noting the wind direction, the pilot rolled out on a final heading, slowed, and touched down cautiously on the ridgeline.

After dropping Lee and Kolby on the ridgeline, H-10 returned to Garden Valley to pick up the two remaining crewmen, Wayne Hamilton and Mike Spiker. They were dropped off at the same helispot (helicopter landing site) and headed downhill to assist Lee and Kolby. The helicopter returned to base at Garden Valley.

The helitack was now out of first response firefighters. Two and a half hours later, the fire along the highway was sufficiently guarded and contained, allowing the four helitack firefighters to be released and transported back to the helibase. After checking equipment and repacking fire packs, they were once again ready to be dispatched to new fires.

At approximately 3:45 p.m., the helibase was notified to have H-10, with a fire crew, to Cook Creek Ridge. This was the same area that Shinrock and Taylor had been helicoptered to the day before. There was confusion on the radios as to what was taking place. Shinrock and Taylor plus the Lowman firefighters had reported their fire controlled, but they were now calling for more help. Whitehawk and Scott Mountain lookouts were reporting a huge column of smoke with fire shooting skyward. The Boise dispatchers were still trying to sort out the situation; it was not clear if this was the same fire or a different one in the same area.

After liftoff, H-10 climbed steadily northeast. It would require climbing from 3,168 feet, Garden Valley's elevation, to over 8,100 feet in order to clear the ridgeline just southeast of Scott Mountain.

The helicopter leveled off above the ridgeline, and the crew could see tongues of flames bursting out of the dense smoke about twenty miles from their position.

The crew at the fire were now saying that they were completely surrounded by fire and were unable to get out, although they still had a pumper truck with them.

The radio traffic became heavier and more confusing. The dispatcher interrupted and ordered silence on that frequency due to the emergency. He was now able to communicate with the trapped firefighters and would be able to determine what course of action to take for their safety.

Ron Lou, the firefighter in charge of the Lowman crew, again radioed that they were unable to escape the fire and were using what little water that was in the pumper to wet themselves down. He requested that the helicopter attempt to fly them out.

H-10 was at maximum power but still six minutes from the fire. Patnaude radioed that he had copied Lou's transmission and that the helicopter would be over the fire in a few minutes.

What would normally have been a small controllable lightning-started fire had turned into a nightmare. The original fire had been controlled, but unbeknownst to the firefighters, one of the dreaded "sleeper" fires had suddenly sprung to life down a tree-covered hill approximately a half mile to the southwest.

Fanned by winds twenty to twenty-five miles per hour, the undetected fire began its race uphill toward the unsuspecting firefighters. As the fire gained in size and fury, it started climbing the trunks of the thick dry pine and fir trees.

As H-10 was approaching the fire, it was decided that Lee and Kolby would be dropped west of the fire on a logging road switchback to put them in a safe area. The normal circling and reconnaissance of the landing site, to check for hazards, was omitted due to critical life-threating circumstances.

H-10 touched down on the curved portion of the logging road. The two firefighters leaped from the helicopter, dragging their packs and equipment with them. In seconds, H-10 was again airborne and back over the fire.

Patnaude made immediate radio contact with Lou and asked for directions to his location. It was impossible to see down into the fire because of the heavy smoke. Lou radioed that he could barely make out a patch of blue sky to the east of their location.

The helicopter quickly skirted the edge of the fire and smoke and was soon on the east side turning back to the west. Lou radioed that he had the helicopter in sight and that it was a little north of his location. Sisk corrected his flight path back to the left, but the trapped men could still not be spotted. He advised Patnaude that the approach would have to be aborted if the men on the ground could not be located. Patnaude unfastened his shoulder harness, opened the door, and leaned out of the helicopter, desperately searching for the trapped firefighters.

Through the smoke, Patnaude was able to spot the pumper truck and then saw the firefighters huddled in front of the truck. He directed the pilot to the left, then through the swirling smoke and debris kicked up by the rotor wash. Sisk pinpointed the logging road and made a steep descent using a single tree by the road as a guide and a means to keep his bearings.

Because of the thick smoke and downwash from the rotor blades, Sisk could only see to his right about thirty to forty feet, barely outside of the helicopter's rotor diameter. He instructed Patnaude to watch the left side and the tail rotor for clearance of trees and any other hazards during the precarious approach. H-10 touched down cautiously on the logging road, the rotor downwash adding a cloud of dust and ashes to the billowing smoke.

Patnaude quickly herded three of the firefighters into the back seats of the Bell Jet Ranger. The firefighters had been advised prior to the extraction that no tools or packs were to be loaded onto the helicopter. The weight with just the firefighters was going to be a critical factor in getting everyone out. With Patnaude back on board, Sisk lifted the helicopter to a hover, concerned about tail rotor clearance, as he made a right 180-degree pedal turn.

The heat from the fire ingested into the air intake of the turbine engine made the engine temperature gauge needle shoot to redline immediately. The winds and turbulence created by the raging fire suddenly spun the helicopter completely around, causing it to settle back toward the ground and become unable to climb the one hundred vertical feet required to clear the burning trees.

The pilot sideslipped H-10 back onto the road, touching down just as the helicopter began another spin and barely missed a burning stump. Reluctantly, one of the firefighters jumped out and ran for the protection of the pumper truck. The truck was becoming a concern now, the heat was beginning to blister the paint, and it wasn't known how much heat the fuel tank could take before it exploded.

Once again, the helicopter lifted off. Again, the engine temperature went to redline, but this time H-10 was climbing slowly up through the dense smoke. In seconds, they broke into blue sky and fresh air. Choking and gasping, the men aboard the helicopter hungrily gulped the clean air into their lungs.

The helicopter started an immediate descent to the logging road a quarter mile south of the fire to drop the firefighters off. Returning to the fire, H-10 again approached from the east and began a descent back into the smoke. Spotting the guide tree, the pilot shot the approach to the same landing spot. Two more firefighters were quickly loaded, and the same departure route was followed. One firefighter, Ron Taylor, remained to be airlifted from the fire.

Patnaude and Sisk made their final approach back into the inferno. The fire and smoke had grown in intensity making it more difficult to see the landing spot. Patnaude was again leaning out of the open door, shouting instructions over the intercom, the roar of the fire and helicopter noise making it difficult to hear. Sisk spotted the now familiar tree and once again landed close by.

Dodging falling, burning debris, Taylor made a run for the helicopter and leaped into the back seat. As if sensing that it had completed its task, the helpful tree suddenly erupted into a flaming torch. H-10 struggled into the air and again the force of the heated wind spun the helicopter around. The tail rotor barely cleared a fully engulfed burning tree, and the paint on the tail boom began to blister from the intense heat.

As the helicopter spun, it was also lifted by the same erratic winds and boosted over the burning trees into the clear. Taylor was reunited with the other firefighters on the logging road. Luckily, the firefighters suffered only slight burns and some smoke inhalation. Lee and Kolby, who had been dropped off in a safe area while the emergency evacuation was ongoing, were picked up and reunited with the rest of their crew. By now, H-10 was critically low on fuel and headed to the Elk Creek Guard Station, a few miles north, for refueling.

Air tanker planes began dropping fire retardant on the raging fire in an attempt to slow its progress. After refueling, H-10 began ferrying newly arrived firefighters from Elk Creek to a safe area near the fire so they could begin a ground attack in conjunction with the aerial assault from the air tankers.

The fire burned out of control for a week, eventually consuming more than seven hundred acres of prime forest. Seven airplanes, three helicopters, and two hundred fifty firefighters finally brought the fire under control.

Firefighter Ron Taylor describes the chain of events sparked by the sleeper fire: "We were mopping up the original fire; this was around 1300 hours. We continued to patrol the fire line and worked on any smokes that were showing up. At about 15:20, I noticed a column of smoke to the southwest and downhill from us. The fire appeared to be moving about fifteen to twenty miles per hour and crowning out. We tried to determine the best course of action for the new fire and decided that a backfire would be the best thing to do. (Author's note: A backfire

Author's file photo of Air Tanker 27.

is another tool used by wildland firefighters. When weather conditions and safety concerns allow, the firefighters can construct a fire line, either by hand tools or bulldozers to clear brush and other flammable fuels at a predetermined location from the approaching wildfire. Once the fire line is constructed, the fuels along the fire line are ignited by hand torches or by aerial ignition utilizing helicopters. As the approaching wildfire nears the fire line, the excessive heat from the wildfire begins drawing cooler air and the backfire inward, thus starving the main fire of fuel.) The Lowman District Office was advised of the situation, but due to misinterpretation and confusion over the two fires, the backfire plan was aborted.

"Within fifteen minutes, the fire was approximately ten acres and moving rapidly. We worked our way back to a small clear-cut area and found that the fire had burned across the logging road and had cut off our way out."

Ron Lou radioed a request for a helicopter evacuation. Ron Taylor's description of the fire continues: "Around 1600 hours, the helicopter arrived on scene. We were completely surrounded by dense smoke and fire. The helicopter made its approach from the east, through a small hole in the smoke. As the pilot settled the helicopter to the ground, a tree next to the tail boom lit off.

"It was very hot and smoky; the bird (helicopter) could only handle two of us at a time, without any of our gear. I was the last man out, and when they came back in for me, it appeared that every tree within a half mile was on fire."

Several weeks later, while en route to another fire, the helitack crew looked down on the havoc that the Cook Creek Ridge Fire had wrought. Everything appeared deathly still. The small clearing and the old logging road where the landings were made were visible. Beside the road stood what was left of the guide tree, now charred black. One twisted, blackened limb reached upward as if gesturing a final farewell.

CHAPTER SEVEN

Mortar Creek Fire

The late July heat spilled over the steep slopes and rushed downward to the Salmon River far below. A gust of hot air swooped low over the cold water of the river. As it tried to displace the thin layer of cool air lying just inches above the swift-moving water, the gust began swirling and, like a school of feeding piranha, worked itself into a mini tornado-like frenzy. Suddenly, the whirlwind skimming the river darted toward the west bank.

Only a few hours earlier, two campers had broken camp after enjoying a leisurely breakfast and hot coffee cooked over an open campfire. The fire was allowed to burn out, and the leftover coffee was dumped over the hot coals.

Anxious to resume their journey down the famous River of No Return, the campers had neglected the standard practices and proper conduct concerning wilderness campfires. A few extra minutes of pouring water and stirring the smoldering ashes would have prevented the chain reaction of disasters that were about to be unleashed.

Reaching the gradual slope of the riverbank, the whirlwind changed directions and moved directly toward the small circle of rocks that had contained the campfire earlier.

As it reached the site, the whirlwind seemed to pause, causing the damp ashes to be sucked into the spinning mass of air. A tiny ember, buried under several inches of damp ashes, was now pulled free and joined the whirlwind that once again began to accelerate north along the riverbank.

The ember, now fanned to a brilliant glow, was flung from the whirlwind and landed in a small tuft of tall dead grass. As if catching its breath, the ember rested momentarily in the grass. A few seconds later, a thin spindly wisp of smoke drifted out of the grass as one stalk pressured by the ember crumbled into ash. Unable to resist the heat, the rest of the grass burst into flame. Just as it was about to die out, a fresh rush of warm air hit the burning grass, blowing it across the footpath and into a larger area of dead grass.

The fire now began to spread in all directions. The hot, dry wind continued to increase and pushed the fire to a clump of dry brush and some dry rotted logs. The brush torched the lower limbs and needles of a pine tree.

Like crepe paper, the pine needles burned rapidly. The fire shot upward, consuming every needle as it reached the top of the tree. The fire, now approximately forty feet above the ground and being fanned by the winds, leaped from treetop to treetop, building an explosive heat as it progressed.

Burning debris from the trees fell back to the ground and, in turn, started new fires that would make a run for more unburned areas. The winds, due to midafternoon heating from the sun, were now approaching twenty-five miles per hour.

The stage was set. Before the destruction and fiery carnage was over, set in place by one little ember, six people would be dead, dozens injured, buildings destroyed or damaged, and 70,000 acres of wilderness would be burned and devastated.

Morehead fire lookout is perched on an isolated knob, a few miles west of the Middle Fork of the Salmon River. Only the love for the beauty of the surrounding mountains and valleys could overcome the vast loneliness for a fire lookout based here. The only way into Morehead is either by foot, packhorse, or helicopter. Communication with

Morehead Lookout. FILE PHOTO COURTESY OF RAY DAVIS.

the outside world is through a two-way radio, tuned to the Fire Dispatch Center in Boise, Idaho, a hundred miles to the south, or an occasional backpacker that might be passing through en route to the Salmon River country.

A few years back, while traveling a narrow trail toward a spring to fetch drinking water, a fire lookout assigned to Morehead rounded a bend, finding himself face-to-face with a mountain lion and her two cubs. Backstepping and trying not to show fear, the lookout was attacked and knocked to the ground. The lion, seeing that her cubs had scurried off, bounded down the trail and out of sight.

The lookout, thoroughly shaken and bleeding profusely from a head laceration, managed to make it back to the lookout tower where he then contacted the ranger station at Cascade, Idaho.

The US Forest Service helicopter, based at Garden Valley, was dispatched to medevac the injured man. After only a few days in the hospital and numerous stitches, the lookout insisted that he return to his lonely post.

The fire, sparked by the whirlwind, had now grown to several acres. The black smoke from the trees that were crowning out was beginning to make its way up and out of the steep canyon. The ground fire continued its march toward more trees, igniting them like torches. The tongues of flame reached skyward, licking at the pine needles and the lower hanging branches, then shooting to the tops.

The Morehead lookout did a double take. He was positive that he had seen smoke, but now he was not sure. The wind had flattened the smoke out again and was pushing it downstream through the canyon. Grabbing the binoculars, the lookout swept slowly back and forth scanning the canyon. "There, it is smoke!" he said aloud.

Swinging the fire spotting instrument around and aligning it toward the fire, he was able to get a compass reading. Unable to see the base of the fire, he would only be able to give an approximate location when he called the report in.

"Boise dispatch, Morehead Lookout, I have a smoke," the lookout radioed.

"Go ahead with your legal, Morehead," responded the dispatcher.

"I can't see the base, but it appears to be in the Middle Fork and in the area of Mortar Creek." The lookout then proceeded to furnish the dispatcher with the other details. He relayed the legal—the compass heading, the approximate distance from Morehead to the fire, and an observation of the weather conditions.

The Boise dispatcher contacted the Garden Valley helitack and directed the helicopter foreman to launch their helicopter immediately. The helicopter, with four men aboard, was airborne within three minutes.

Fifteen minutes later, the helitack foreman radioed the lookout on Morehead, asking for a compass heading. "Never mind, Morehead. We have the smoke in sight. It looks like it is really cooking," he commented.

"Helicopter-10, give me an assessment of your needs when you are over the fire," the Boise dispatcher transmitted. The helicopter approached the fire from the south and a thousand feet above the Salmon River. Orbiting the fire in a counterclockwise flight path, the helitack foreman was getting an accurate map location and an estimate of the size and potential of the wildfire.

"Boise dispatch, we have about five acres burning at this time. It's crowning out and we have winds at twenty to twenty-five knots," the foreman relayed. "The fire is on the west side of the river but will probably jump the river with this wind," he added.

"What kind of resources do you need?" asked the dispatcher.

"Well, the fire is rolling through the top of the trees. I don't think firefighters on the ground will help right now, nor would it be safe," said the foreman. "If we could get some retardant drops in there, it might keep the fire from jumping the river."

"Standby, Helicopter-10." A few minutes later the dispatcher was back on the radio. "Negative on the air drops. All of the air tankers are committed to other fires at this time."

Sixty miles north, the Ship Island Creek Fire was raging out of control. Airtankers and smokejumpers were trying to assist the firefighters already on the fire, but they were having high wind problems also. There were deep concerns about the firefighters' safety.

"Helicopter-10, contact the Indian Creek ranger on the Challis frequency," the Boise dispatcher radioed. The Indian Creek Guard Station and airstrip was downriver about six miles from the fire that the helicopter was orbiting. The Middle Fork of the Salmon River is the boundary line separating the Boise National Forest and the Challis National Forest.

The ranger at Indian Creek had been advised of the fire upriver and was en route along the hiking trail by horseback. The ranger's main concern was the safety of the rafters that were floating the river and of the few people that were living and camping at another remote airstrip called Pistol Creek.

"Indian Creek, this is Helicopter-10."

"Go ahead 10," answered the ranger on his portable radio. He had stopped on a small sandbar in midstream when he heard the helicopter approaching. After dismounting, he kept a firm grip on the horse's reins and lead line, anticipating that the helicopter might spook the horse.

INDIAN CREEK S81 INDIAN CREEK

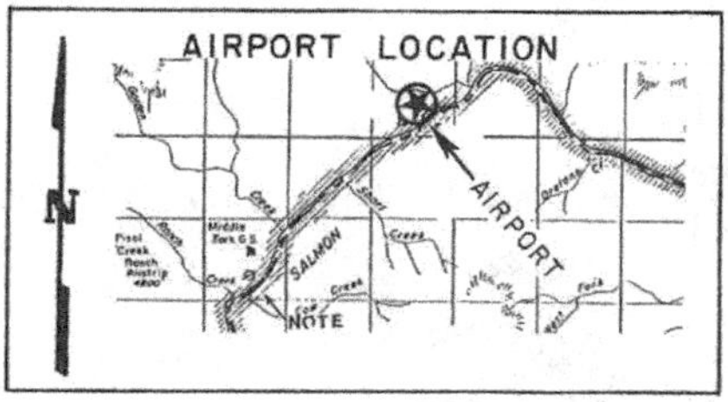

LAT 44° 45.7′ N

LONG 115° 06.4′ W

VOR	FREQ	RAD	NM
LKT	113.5	231°	50 NM

FSS BOISE (BOI) 1-800-632-6582

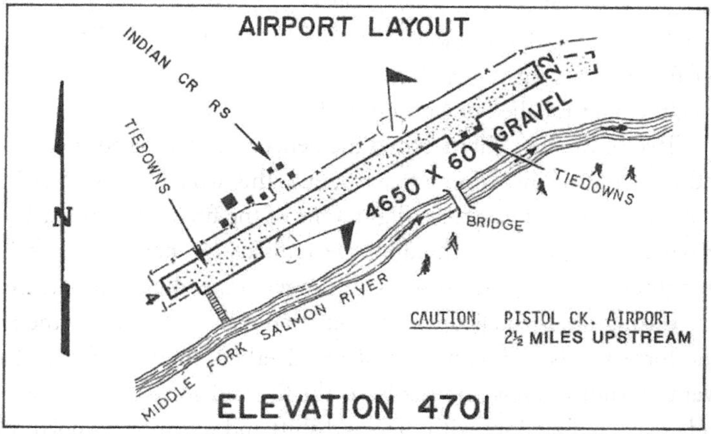

LOCATION: ADJACENT SE R.S.

FUEL: NO

LIGHTS: NO

COMMUNICATION: CTAF: 122.9
FSS: 121.1T, 113.5R

REMARKS:
CAUTION: OTHER AIRPORT TRAFFIC CONFINED TO SAME CANYON AREA. SPECIAL CONSIDERATION SHOULD BE GIVEN TO DENSITY ALTITUDE, TURBULENCE, AND MOUNTAIN FLYING PROFICIENCY. PISTOL CREEK AIRPORT LOCATED 2.5 MILES UPSTREAM. USFS RECOMMENDS REMAIN IN MAIN CANYON WHEN DEPARTING UP OR DOWNSTREAM. DO NOT ATTEMPT TO CLIMB OUT SIDE CANYONS. CLOSE FLIGHT PLAN PRIOR TO LANDING. NO WINTER MAINTENANCE.

"We are looking for you. What's your location?"

"About a mile downstream on a sandbar. If you can land, I would like to get in and make a recon of the fire," explained the ranger.

Indian Creek Airstrip. PHOTOGRAPH COURTESY OF THE US FOREST SERVICE.

The helicopter crew spotted the ranger and horse. Making a tight 180-degree turn back into the wind, now blowing fiercely straight down the river, the pilot touched down cautiously on the sandbar.

Two of the firefighters exited the helicopter and pulled their packs and tools out of the cargo compartment. This would lighten the helicopter for the reconnaissance flight. One of the firefighters trotted over to where the ranger was holding the reins of the nervous horse. The firefighter held onto the horse as the ranger climbed into the backseat.

Lifting off, the helicopter was buffeted back and forth by the near gale force winds. Climbing out of the riverbed, the aircraft was back over the wildfire a few minutes later. The fire had gotten much worse. It had changed directions with the wind shift and was moving northward but was still on the west side of the river.

After a quick orbit of the fire, the ranger decided that it would be suicidal to attempt to fight the fire with ground personnel at this time. The fire was moving rapidly downstream toward the two firefighters and horse waiting on the sandbar. It was time to get everyone out of the area.

As the helicopter headed back to the sandbar, the radio silence was suddenly interrupted by the Boise dispatcher's voice calling Helicopter-10. There was a sound of concern and urgency in his normally calm and professional voice.

"H-10, do not put anyone on that fire! Do you copy? Do not put anyone on the fire!" he repeated. The helicopter foreman acknowledged the order. The dispatcher continued, "We have just lost two firefighters at Ship Island Creek! We are pulling everyone back!"

The Ship Island Creek Fire had erupted into an uncontrollable nightmare. The same erratic winds that were playing havoc with the Mortar Creek Fire had sent the Ship Island Creek Fire rushing in all directions. The firefighters on the fire were fleeing for their lives.

Two of the firefighters scrambled desperately uphill trying to reach the safety of a small clearing that had been used earlier as a spike camp.

Gasping for air and choking on the heavy smoke, the men quickly unrolled their emergency fire resistance shelters and began digging shallow trenches. They were out of time; they burrowed into the depressions, pulling the fire shelters over themselves and tucking it in on all sides.

A solid wall of fire roared toward the clearing. Like a gigantic monster gone completely berserk, the fire consumed everything in its path. The intense heat caused trees to explode like popcorn kernels, thrusting flaming debris high into the air and out ahead of the main fire.

The fire barely slowed for the clearing. Stockpiled supplies that had been delivered to the spike camp earlier burst into flame, consuming everything. The fire quickly gobbled up what little oxygen there was. Toxic smoke from the plastic water containers and the burning camping gear drifted under the firefighters' shelters. The odds were too great, and the firefighters would not win this battle against a relentless foe.

Helicopter-10 landed back at the sandbar. The ranger, mounted on his horse, headed north on the trail at a quickened pace. After picking up the two firefighters and their equipment, the helicopter departed south following the river.

The plan was to fly just above the water and to attempt to warn anyone floating the river about the wildfire. Rounding a bend, the helicopter crew was suddenly upon the fire. It had jumped across the river and was burning furiously on both sides.

Middle Fork of the Salmon River. PHOTOGRAPH COURTESY OF THE US FOREST SERVICE.

Because of the erratic winds and the narrowness of the canyon, Helicopter-10 was unable to turn around. The only way out was through the gauntlet of fire. It was like flying through a tunnel. The inside of the helicopter glowed a bright flickering orange. The reddish faces of the four crewmen were grim with concern.

A blizzard of burning pine needles flowed past the windshield. In a few minutes, they were through the worst of the fire and began climbing above the riverbed. A mile upstream from the fire, the helicopter crew spotted the first of several rafts. Six or more people occupied each raft as they floated casually downriver and unsuspectingly toward the inferno.

After landing on a small sandbar littered with river rocks, Patnaude quickly exited the helicopter and began waving frantically to the lead raft to come ashore. The rafters beached the rafts as the helicopter foreman explained the situation and danger taking place ahead. The fire had consumed the base of numerous dead snags, causing the flaming dead trees to fall crashing into and, in some cases, completely across the river, creating an extremely hazardous condition for anyone attempting to traverse the river by raft.

Helicopter-10 continued flying upriver, stopping several more times to warn rafting parties of the wildfire. As the fuel was getting low, the helicopter crew returned to the Garden Valley Helibase to prepare for the busy day that the following morning would bring.

The rafters would be unable to continue their trip for several days. In the meantime, the Forest Service had closed that section of river from Boundary Creek downstream to Indian Creek.

By 11:00 p.m., the unchecked fire had burned an estimated 1,400 acres on both sides of the Middle Fork of the Salmon. A fixed-wing aircraft equipped with infrared cameras was scheduled to fly over the fire at 2:00 a.m. The photos would give a more accurate evaluation of the acres burned and show the direction the fire was moving.

Throughout the night, firefighters and equipment were being mobilized at the Boise Interagency Fire Center. Bruce Meadows, a large open area with a US Forest Service grass airstrip, was designated as the base fire camp where all the operations and the upcoming battle with the Mortar Creek Fire would be conducted from. Because of the inaccessibility and lack of roads, the entire movement of firefighters and supplies would have to be done with aircraft.

Firefighters who had been held in reserve or who had been released from other fires were quickly reorganized and loaded on buses at Boise for the long arduous five-hour trip over mountainous roads to the staging area at Bruce Meadows. A large number of helicopters would be required to transport firefighters and equipment the twenty air miles from Bruce Meadows to the fire.

A call went out from the fire center across the country for any available aircraft. Many of the qualified firefighting helicopters were already committed to other fires throughout the West.

As the gearing up to attack the Mortar Creek Fire continued, approximately twenty miles west of the fire in the treacherous mountains surrounding Thunderbolt Lookout, four more fires burst into life.

Smokejumpers based in McCall, Idaho, parachuted into the rugged wilderness and snuffed the fires out before they could grow.

After several days of persistent work and with cooperation from the weather, the Mortar Creek firefighters, with the help from airtankers and helicopters dropping fire retardant and water, began to slow the advance of the fire and were progressing with building fire lines. The fire had now been burning for a week and had destroyed over 2,200 acres of forest.

In a resurgence of fury, driven by winds more than thirty miles per hour, the fire exploded across the constructed fire lines and roared once again out of control. In just one day, the fire had consumed an additional 4,800 acres, bringing the total acres destroyed to 7,000. A Red Flag Warning was put into effect for the whole area. The Red Flag Warning is a special alert of extremely hazardous conditions with severe dryness and high winds. Thunderstorms with dry lightning are often included in the warnings.

The main body of the fire was now moving in a southeasterly direction, on the east side of the Middle Fork of the Salmon River. That portion of the fire on the west side was also still raging out of control.

A few days later, on August 4, disaster struck once again. The section of river from Boundary Creek downstream to Indian Creek was still closed to all public access. However, rafting parties could begin their float trip at the Indian Creek launch site. The only way into Indian Creek currently was by air. The landing strip was an improved grass runway and capable of handling various types of light, single- and multi-engine aircraft.

Shortly after 8:00 a.m. at the airport in Boise, the temperature was already approaching 70 degrees Fahrenheit. Several charter aircraft had departed Boise en route to the Indian Creek airstrip, carrying members of a rafting party. Max Sanborn taxied his single-engine airplane out to the active runway and performed his engine run-up checklist. Announcing to the Boise tower that he was ready for departure, Sanborn was given clearance for takeoff.

After takeoff, the Cessna 210 turned northbound and climbed steadily toward the rugged Idaho wilderness looming in the distance. The five passengers chatted casually, excited by anticipation of the forthcoming float trip. The eighty-five-mile trip would take approximately forty minutes. Due to the air restrictions over the Mortar Creek Fire, the charter aircraft inbound to the Indian Creek airstrip would have to deviate slightly to the west to avoid the firefighting aircraft.

After raging all day, the fire would begin to calm as nightfall approached and as the winds began to subside. By early morning, the heated smoke had settled and drifted back down toward the cooler air deep in the main canyon of the Middle Fork and then into the smaller tributaries to the river. Flying above the canyons and looking down on the whitish smoke just at daybreak gave the impression that someone had spilled a gigantic bottle of milk, leaving only the highest ridges and peaks thrusting through.

The dense smoke had drifted downstream to the small airstrip at Pistol Creek and was approaching Indian Creek, about a mile further north. Every so often, a boiling column of black smoke would burst through the layer of the calm white carpet of smoke. Far below, a clump of trees, no longer able to withstand the intense ground fire, would explode into flame, sending the black smoke spiraling skyward.

Helicopter-10 departed the Bruce Meadows fire camp to conduct an early morning reconnaissance flight with the fire incident commander and his assistants on board. The purpose for the flight was to determine whether the smoke had cleared sufficiently to allow the helicopters to land and takeoff safely while transporting the day shift of firefighters into the various helispots and to bring the night shift crew back to base camp. The recon would also help determine if the fire had spotted out ahead of the main fire and created potential problem areas that could endanger the firefighters.

Meanwhile, after arriving over the Indian Creek area, Sanborn activated the landing gear lever but was not getting an indication that the wheels were down and locked. Sanborn radioed another aircraft that was in the area and asked the pilot to do a visual check on the gear. The other pilot confirmed that the landing gear was down and appeared to be locked in place.

Shortly after the radio conversation between the two aircraft, Sanborn flew into a dead-end canyon with walls towering two thousand feet. Perhaps because of the concern and distraction over the landing gear and the reduced visibility due to the smoke, Sanborn had inadvertently turned up the wrong canyon while descending for the Indian Creek landing strip.

Helicopter-10 was about to complete the reconnaissance flight of the fire when an urgent call came over the VHF radio frequency. "Forest Service helicopter over the Mortar Creek Fire! Do you copy?"

"This is Helicopter-10, go ahead," the pilot answered.

"If you guys hurry, you might be able to stop another fire. An airplane just crashed in a canyon a couple of miles southwest of Indian Creek, and it's on fire!" the airplane pilot transmitted.

The fire boss on board H-10 immediately radioed the base camp at Bruce Meadows and requested firefighters and rescue personnel to be dispatched to the scene of the crash. A standby helicopter with several firefighters was launched from the fire camp. A smokejumper plane was also dispatched and en route from the jumper base at McCall, Idaho.

Because of the rugged terrain and the dense timber, it was impossible for the rescue helicopter to find a landing spot near the crashed plane. The fire was gaining in size, and the helicopter rescue crew requested a retardant drop to slow the fire until they could get firefighters and rescue people on the ground.

An airtanker arrived and made two drops to slow the fire. In the meantime, the smokejumper plane arrived on scene, and six smokejumpers jumped into the treacherous canyon.

Some of the jumpers pulled Sanborn from the wreckage and began administering medical aid. He was still alive but in critical condition with burns covering 70 percent of his body. The five passengers on board were all deceased. The other smokejumpers worked feverishly to control the fire in the potentially explosive canyon.

During the process of fighting the fire, two smokejumpers were injured. Smokejumper Tom French was transported to Saint Alphonsus Hospital in Boise with a leg injury. He was treated and released later that day and then flown back to the jumper base at McCall.

Unable to find a suitable helicopter landing site nearby, the smokejumpers were able to fell trees and clear a spot approximately a mile from the crash site. Several EMTs were flown into the landing zone to assist with rescue and treatment of the injured pilot.

After several hours of arduous hiking and carrying Sanborn on a litter, the jumpers and EMTs arrived at the helicopter landing site and quickly loaded Sanborn onto the helicopter.

In less than fifteen minutes, the helicopter landed at Bruce Meadows where the smokejumper DC-3 was standing by waiting to transport the critically injured Sanborn to Boise.

En route to Boise, the EMTs and smokejumpers worked desperately to keep Sanborn alive and to keep him from going into shock. They poured water from their canteens on the severe burns, trying to keep moisture on the damaged skin tissues.

Sanborn was conscious and aware of the dramatic effort that the jumpers, medical technicians, and aircrews were providing to help him. Robert (Bobby) Montoya, a smokejumper, spoke soothingly trying to reassure Sanborn that he would soon be at the hospital and that everything would be fine. Despite the severe pain, Sanborn spoke. "I will pray for you smokejumpers," he told Montoya. Here was a man fighting for his life, but because of his appreciation and respect for his rescuers, he was praying for their safety. Montoya turned his head as tears welled in his eyes and spilled down his cheeks.

Because of the severity of his burns, Sanborn was flown from Boise to the burn center at the University of Utah Medical Center in Salt Lake City. Despite a massive effort to save his life, Max Sanborn succumbed to his injuries the following day.

CHAPTER EIGHT

Harrah's Lodge

The Mortar Creek Fire continued unchecked, consuming thousands of acres of forest each day. The firefighters made progress only to have erratic winds send the fire boiling over the fire lines. The fire had now destroyed over 40,000 acres.

Approximately eight miles east of Pistol Creek, the fire was approaching Harrah's Lodge, a guest and tourist retreat located at the confluence of Thomas Creek and the Middle Fork of the Salmon River.

It was decided to attempt a helicopter lift of firefighters into the lodge area. The smoke was so thick that the helicopters would have to fly low, down the Middle Fork, to reach the lodge.

For most of the helicopter pilots, veterans of the Vietnam War, the low-level flight would be reminiscent of the tactics used against another foe years earlier. In trail formation, the helicopters wove their way downriver, sometimes flying only slightly faster than a hover.

Breaking into the clearing, the helicopters touched down at Thomas Creek airstrip adjacent to the lodge. The twenty-person firefighting team went to work immediately, clearing brush, setting up pumps and fire hoses, and preparing for the worst. A number of guests, upon learning of the approaching fire, quickly loaded their belongings into their rafts and departed downriver to escape the fire.

Middle Fork Lodge. PHOTOGRAPH COURTESY OF THE MIDDLE FORK LODGE.

The firefighters decided to backfire the area around the lodge and several other outbuildings. Time was running out. The roar of the approaching fire could be detected, although it was still a half mile away.

A pumper unit began drawing water from the river and started wetting down the buildings. Heat from the fire, now only an eighth of a mile away, could be felt by the Harrah's employees and the firefighters. Visibility was now less than a hundred feet.

The backfire was working. The flames ate hungrily at the dry fuels. As the hot, main fire drew closer, it began pulling the backfire toward it, thus consuming the fuels away from the lodge and the surrounding buildings. It was a classic example of fighting fire with fire.

The lodge and resort compound were spared, but the Mortar Creek Fire raged on. It was far from being over.

CHAPTER NINE

Blowup on the West Side

That portion of the fire on the west side of the river, the side the fire had originally started on, had not been a major problem after the first few days. Because of the direction of the winds, the main fire had jumped the river and was being pushed to the east and northeast. The west side fire was still a threat, however, and sooner or later, action would have to be taken to battle it.

With the arrival of more firefighters at the base camp, the helitack crew from Garden Valley and their Helicopter-10 would now be available for initial attack on any new fires that might start in the Boise National Forest, their area of responsibility. However, they would still be based at the Bruce Meadows fire camp and airstrip.

In the meantime, the helitack crew were assigned the task of clearing helicopter landing spots on the western portion of the Mortar Creek Fire. Once the landing spots were cleared, fire crews would be flown in, and they would begin the job of constructing fire lines to try and contain that part of the fire. Two helitack firefighters, Taylor and Lee, were dropped off on a finger ridge, west and uphill of the fire, and began constructing a suitable helispot.

While the two men labored in the midday heat, Helicopter-10 was dispatched with two firefighters, the helitack foreman, and a pilot aboard to take the initial attack on a new lightning-started fire. This fire was located west of Mortar Creek, in the Forest Service's Landmark Camp area.

The afternoon winds had started increasing again, but this time something was different. The hot winds were blowing out of the east. This helped slow the advance of the main fire by blowing it back toward the previously burned areas. On the west side, however, the wind began pushing the fire uphill and out of the canyon toward dry, unburned timber and ground fuels.

The two helitack crewmen constructing the helispot had noticed the wind shift and were keeping a cautious eye on the smoke billowing up from the canyon below. Taylor had been the last firefighter out of the Cook Creek Ridge Fire only a few weeks earlier. He did not want to go through another ordeal like that one.

A short time later, Lee radioed the communications center at Bruce Meadows, requesting that they be extracted by helicopter. He also stated that the fire on the west side was increasing in size and headed uphill toward his and Taylor's location. The communications center told the crew to stand by. A few minutes later, they radioed Lee that they were trying to break a helicopter away from another mission and that they would send it for them shortly.

The crew on board Helicopter-10 had been monitoring the radio conversation between Lee and the communication center while en route to the new fire. Ray Patnaude, the foreman on board, radioed communications that they could divert to Lee and Taylor's location and pick them up. Patnaude was told to continue to the new fire start and that another helicopter would make the extraction.

Back at Bruce Meadows, fire operations radioed Lee and Taylor to check on their status. "We are still hiking up the finger ridge. We have abandoned our tools and are attempting to outrun the fire," Lee radioed back, out of breath. Patnaude and the pilot on Helicopter-10 had heard enough; it was their crew down there in trouble.

The pilot turned the helicopter back toward the ridge, where a huge cloud of black, billowing smoke was shooting skyward. The crew on the helicopter searched desperately for a landing spot where they could drop the two firefighters in the back seat in a safe location. Toward the highest part of the same finger ridge, they saw an old helispot. There was brush growing on the old spot, but the pilot thought the helicopter could be landed safely without the tail rotor hitting the brush.

The helicopter landed and the two firefighters quickly exited, taking their packs and tools with them. Helicopter-10 departed and headed directly down the ridge to find Lee and Taylor, who were now running for their lives.

In a few minutes, the two helitack crewmen were located. They were struggling to climb over a rock outcropping; the going was painfully slow. Just above the rocks, however, was a small clearing. The helicopter would not be able to land because of the steep slope of the terrain, but they would be able to get the aircraft into the clearing.

The plan was to orbit until the men on the ground were in place at the clearing. The helicopter would then approach the clearing, crossways of the ridgeline. The pilot would very carefully touch the uphill skid of the helicopter to the sloped ground and hold that position while the two firefighters climbed into the back seats.

On the verge of exhaustion, the firefighters finally reached the small clearing. Hunkering down where they determined the center of the clearing was, the two men waited as Helicopter-10 rolled out on a final approach to the spot.

Approaching the helispot from north to south, the pilot would be dealing with a crosswind. The same gusting winds driving the fire up the ridge were buffeting H-10 as the helicopter touched the right skid to the ground. The pilot would have to hold the helicopter in this position long enough for the two firefighters to open the right rear door and then slide in carefully so that the pilot could compensate for the added weight and balance of the aircraft. The first firefighter opened the door and held it as the other man stepped onto the skid and then eased into the back seat. Without hesitation, he carefully slid over to the center seat. The firefighter holding the door then stepped up and into the helicopter, settling into the outside seat. As he was shutting the door, the first man in now slid over to the left, far side seat. The helicopter was now evenly balanced with the weight equally distributed. During the extraction, as each person was entering the helicopter, the pilot was continuously making corrections with the controls to hold the aircraft in the same place. The helicopter was still flying but with one skid lightly touching the ground and holding in one place, while still compensating for the upslope wind.

The whole crew extraction, after touching the uphill skid to the ground, took less than sixty seconds to complete. The highly trained helitack crew knew exactly how to perform this dangerous maneuver. H-10 lifted off and did a pedal turn into the wind. This would aid the pilot in getting airborne. It would also require flying directly into the smoke from the fire, but only for a short time to build up airspeed. After gaining airspeed and translational lift, the pilot turned the helicopter south into fresh air.

The concern now was to get the two firefighters who were dropped off earlier off the ridge and out of the path of the advancing fire. Patnaude was in radio contact with the fire camp at Bruce Meadows. The dispatcher said that another helicopter was en route to assist with the pickup of the crew. If the helicopter did not arrive within fifteen minutes, the fire would be closing in on those two firefighters—a repeat of what had just taken place farther down the ridge.

H-10 was not going to leave until the two firefighters were safely off the ridge. The helicopter was not configured to carry six people, but if the other chopper did not arrive in time, H-10 would make the attempt to get the men out, even if it meant that they would have to ride the skids. Orbiting over the helispot, H-10 was burning fuel, and this was helping to lessen the weight. The weight of the aircraft and the four men on board would be a critical factor in being able to lift off from the spot with two more people.

Just as the crew were preparing to start their approach to the landing spot, the other helicopter radioed that they were only a few minutes out and asked the pilot of H-10 to guide them in once he had them spotted. A few seconds later, the pilot of the incoming helicopter radioed that he had the orbiting H-10 in sight and was heading directly to their location.

The two firefighters on the ground had used their time while waiting for pickup to improve the helispot and to clear any brush and obstacles that would be hazardous to the tail rotor of the helicopter. H-10 had climbed to a higher altitude to give the other helicopter plenty of room to make the extraction.

The helicopter touched down easily on the well-cleared landing zone. The firefighters loaded their equipment in the cargo hold and then boarded the helicopter. Lifting off, the helicopter joined up with H-10, and both ships flew back to Bruce Meadows for some much-needed rest and medical checkups for the two firefighters who had come close to getting trapped by the fire.

The Mortar Creek Fire would continue to burn for several more weeks. It would be months before it was declared fully extinguished. This would only happen after cooler temperatures, rainfall, and even snowfall would finally bring the tragic fire to an end.

CHAPTER TEN

Sorrow on Storm King Mountain

July 6, 1994, was the fourth day since the South Canyon Fire was ignited by a lightning strike. At the day's end, fourteen wildland firefighters would perish, and others would suffer severe burns and injuries.

Storm King Mountain is located five miles northwest of Glenwood Springs, Colorado, and just north of Interstate 70 and the Colorado River.

The Bureau of Land Management's (BLM) Grand Junction District was coping with extreme fire conditions due to near record-high temperatures from the previous month. The number of fires was twice the annual average. At the time the South Canyon Fire started, the Grand Junction District was dealing with more than forty other fires, most started by lightning storms. Priority for attacking the fires was given to protecting residences, structures, and utilities, and to those fires that had the most potential for rapid spread.

According to the South Canyon Fire investigation report, at 11:00 a.m. on July 3, the Garfield County Sheriff reported the fire to the Grand Junction District dispatch center. A BLM engine crew E611 arrived at the scene and met with the sheriff. The engine foreman completed the initial size-up and confirmed the fire was on BLM-administered land.

The South Canyon fire at noon on July 4. PHOTOGRAPH COURTESY OF THE US FOREST SERVICE.

With only the flaming canopies of two trees visible, this fire seemed to have a low spread potential. The engine foreman recommended that the fire be observed until firefighting resources could be obtained. There were higher priority fires, the slopes were steep, the fire was inaccessible, and rates of spread were slow.

On July 4, five new fires were started—two that exceeded one hundred acres. Thirty-one of the previous fires remained uncontrolled, and more lightning was forecast for that evening. Red Flag Warnings were issued.

Due to concerns of Glenwood Springs residents, the South Canyon Fire was given a higher priority. At 2:50 p.m., the White River National Forest, Sopris Ranger District, informed the Grand Junction District dispatch that it had received a telephone call from a resident concerned about the fire, and in response, it was sending an engine crew to the fire site.

At 3:40 p.m., Sopris Ranger District reported to dispatch that the fire posed no danger to structures. Dispatch responded that a BLM engine crew was en route to the fire site.

At 6:30 p.m., the incident commander, the BLM, and Forest Service firefighters met at the bottom of the hill. They sized up the fire and decided that because of darkness and steep terrain, they would hike up to attack the fire early on July 5.

The Bureau of Land Management and the US Forest Service jointly investigated this tragic loss of life and chain of events leading up to the accident. Because of the number of fatalities and the workplace hazards and environment, the federal agency Occupational Safety and Health Administration, known as OSHA, also conducted an in-depth investigation.

From the Executive Summary of OSHA's Investigation of the South Canyon Fire report, they summarized the events leading into the catastrophe, beginning with the BLM and Forest Service crews arriving at the location just off Interstate 70 below the fire:

THE ACCIDENT:

On July 2, 1994, lightning ignited a single tree on Bureau of Land Management land approximately seven miles west of Glenwood Springs, Colorado. The fire started at an elevation of approximately 7000 feet on a ridge in extremely steep, mountainous terrain. Fuel in the vicinity consisted of juniper–pinion mix with dense stands of Gambel oak. There was some grass ground cover. Fuel moisture was very low as a result of prolonged drought conditions in the area.

On July 4, a Forest Service/Bureau of Land Management team of seven firefighters arrived on Interstate 70 below the fire but did not begin actual firefighting operations as it was late in the day and there was an arduous 2 ½ hour hike to the fire site. A Red Flag Warning was issued by the National Weather Service. Fire size at this time was three to four acres.

The seven firefighters, led by a Bureau of Land Management Incident Commander, hiked to the fire the following day and began fire suppression activities which included cutting a helicopter landing site, or "Helispot," and constructing a fire line. A Red Flag Warning was again issued. Also on July 5, eight Smoke jumpers from Montana parachuted to the fire site and helped with the fireline construction. The original fireline was overrun by advancing fire so a second line was begun. The Forest Service/Bureau of Land Management team hiked down the mountain that evening to conduct equipment repairs. The eight Smokejumpers continued to fight the fire until falling rocks forced them to cease firefighting operations and find a safe place to sleep on the mountain until morning. By this time the fire had grown to fifty acres.

On July 6, Red Flag Warnings were again issued by the National Weather Service along with a forecast of the passing cold front accompanied by the shifting and gusting winds. The Forest Service/Bureau of Land Management team hiked back to the fire site early in the morning to rejoin the Smoke jumpers and construct a second helispot (Helispot 2). By noon, the Smoke jumpers and the joint Forest Service/Bureau of Land Management team were joined by the ten Hotshot firefighters from Oregon who arrived by helicopter to Helispot 2. Winds were gusting at up to thirty miles per hour by 1:00 p.m., and the fire, which had expanded to over 150 acres, was burning erratically, with frequent spotting across the firelines, tree torching, and re-burning of some areas. At 3:00 p.m., ten more Oregon Hotshots arrived at Helispot 2. Many of the firefighters were engaged in downhill (fireline) construction. The cold front moved through the area at 3:20 p.m., with strong winds gusting to forty-five miles per hour. The fire activity immediately intensified with flame heights reaching 100 feet. Between 3:30 p.m. and 4:30 p.m., the fire reached "blow-up" proportions. Driven by strong winds, fueled by tinder-dry vegetation, and magnified by the steep terrain, the fire spotted below the firefighters and raced up the hill at a speed of nearly twenty miles per hour with flame lengths reaching 300 feet. Of the forty-nine firefighters on the mountain at the time of the blow-up, fourteen (thirteen from the Forest Service and one Bureau of Land Management) were unable to reach safety and were overcome by the fire. The other thirty-five firefighters barely escaped with their lives.

CHAPTER ELEVEN

Mobilizing for Battle

Early morning on July 5: The morning briefing at the Western Slope Fire Coordination Center called for Red Flag Warnings and very high to extreme fire danger.

After hiking to the fire from the east drainage, the seven BLM firefighters began the construction and clearing for Helispot 1 on the ridge above the fire. From the helispot, they began constructing a direct fire line downhill along the fire's edge. Butch Blanco, the incident commander, requested more firefighters. He also asked for a helicopter along with a twenty-person crew. The twenty firefighters were not available at this time, but a load of eight smokejumpers were dispatched to the fire.

Blanco requested air tanker drops to slow the fire while waiting for additional crews to arrive. The first tanker drop started at H-1 and followed the fire line downhill. Because of the steepness of the terrain and the gusting winds, the Incident Commander (IC) and tanker pilot agreed that more drops would not be effective. The second tanker dropped the retardant south of the fire along the rocky ridge just above Interstate 70. The possibility of falling rocks onto the interstate restricted further use of the air tankers.

At 5:30 p.m., after working all day on building the fire line and Helispot 1, Blanco and his crew began the hike down the canyon to the interstate. Both chainsaws had broken, and the plan was to pull off the fire, do equipment repair, and return to the fire the next day. While they were hiking out at 5:45 p.m., the planeload of eight smokejumpers arrived over the fire. Blanco made radio contact with Sean Cross, the smokejumper spotter, and briefed him on the fire line they had worked on. He told Cross they were headed off the fire and would be back the following day.

First Load of Smokejumpers Jump the Fire

Sean Cross was preparing to parachute to the fire. From Cross's witness statement taken from Appendix 5 in the accident investigation team's report, he describes the flight and arrival over the South Canyon Fire:

> *At 1722 hours on 7-5-94 I departed the Grand Junction Airport as the smoke jumper spotter on BLM jumpship N490AS (DHC-6 Twin Otter) to Grand Junction BLM District fire V-891. On board were eight smoke jumpers, one spotter, and one pilot (Kevin Stalder). We carried 3.5 hours of fuel. ETE to the fire was 25 minutes.*

Plane that dropped the first load of jumpers on July 5. File photo.

Twenty minutes out from the fire, Stalder and I spoke to the pilot of Tanker 127 on VHF 122.925. T127 was inbound to GJT (Grand Junction Airport) after dropping retardant on fire V-891. He told us that terrain was steep at the fire, that he was doubtful as to the effectiveness of the retardant due to that, and that we might have a hard time finding a place to drop jumpers. We thanked him for the information. I told Kevin that if we could not find a suitable place to drop the jumpers we could suggest landing at the Glenwood airport so that the jumpers could reach the fire by ground.

Ten minutes out from the fire I established radio contact with fire IC Butch Blanco. I learned from him that he had 15 firefighters on the fire, that the fire was not rolling or posing too much of a problem at that time, but that both the chainsaws he had were down indefinitely. He said he could use the eight jumpers if we could find a place to drop them. I told Blanco that I would raise him once we were over the fire.

At 1745 490AS arrived over the fire. The fire was 20–30 acres, there was almost no wind on it, and it seemed to be backing down slowly into the drainages on the east and west sides, and down the spur ridge that ran to the southwest off the main knob that the fire was on. After about six passes around the area at about 1500 feet AGL (above ground level) above the fire, Stalder and I determined that we could put the jumpers into a saddle on the same ridgeline as the fire, about 1/4 to 1/2 mile north if the wind conditions were satisfactory. We had only one pattern choice due to terrain considerations, but we felt that it would be sufficient for both jumpers and cargo. I briefed Blanco on what we were going to attempt and, after clearing it with Grand Junction dispatch went to the back of the plane to begin smoke jumper operations.

In the back of the plane, I asked Stalder for a 500 feet AGL observation pass. I used this to determine whether there was turbulence near the ground and to look over the jump spot with Mackey, who was the first in the door. To further reconfirm that Mackey and I were looking at the same jump spot, we made a second pass at 500 feet.

After climbing to 1500 feet, initial streamers showed that we would need to fly a downwind (nonstandard) pattern. Check streamers indicated that winds were very light. Smoke from the fire, which was rising straight up and then drifting slightly to the west, also indicated light winds.

Mackey and I decided the winds were acceptable, and after one more pass to hook up Mackey and Doehring and give them a prejump briefing, they exited the plane. Mackey landed exactly where we had planned, and Doehring, though slightly long, was right in the ballpark. I had told Mackey that I would wait to hear from him on the jumper air/ground FM frequency before dropping the rest of the jumpers. He called me shortly after hitting the ground and confirmed that the spot and conditions were acceptable. He told me there was hardly any wind on the ground but that the jumpers should hold up high. Mackey said that the exit point was acceptable. I relayed this information to the subsequent sticks (teams of two jumpers) during their prejump briefings. The remaining six jumpers reached the ground safely and in the general area of the selected jump site.

Cargo operations took six passes and went smoothly, and by 1840 hours all the jumpers and cargo were on the ground.

Stalder climbed to 1500 feet and continued to circle the area as I waited for Mackey to establish contact with Blanco on the BLM FM frequency. Mackey's radio was giving him difficulty as he was trying to program the new frequency, so I asked Blanco if he could raise Mackey on the jumper air/ground frequency, which he did almost immediately. As soon as contact was established Mackey and Blanco immediately began talking about how to put out the fire.

It was determined that Mackey's crew would head up the ridge to the fireline and begin cutting direct line to the right, or west, toward Blanco's crew. Blanco reminded me that both his saws were out of commission and that he would be pulling his crew out, but that they would be back in the morning. I told him that I thought Mackey's crew should be able to make excellent progress by morning. I told Blanco that I thought the fire looked like it could be caught, but that it could become a problem if it got into the drainage bottoms.

At this time, the fire appeared fairly calm. There was almost no wind on it, and no active flame that I could see from the air. The fire was backing down slowly into the drainages, and although the terrain was steep and the brush heavy in places, I thought it could be caught.

I contacted Mackey and Blanco and told them that 490AS was leaving the area. I contacted Grand Junction dispatch, gave them an update of the jumper status on the fire, and headed back to Grand Junction.

This concluded Sean Cross's narrative and description of the first smokejumper insertion into the South Canyon Fire on July 5. More jumpers and firefighters would be mobilized and committed the following day.

After the jumper and cargo drop operation was completed, Mackey was in radio contact with Blanco. Because Blanco and his crew had already started hiking out to the highway, he advised Mackey that they had begun handline construction from H-1 downhill toward the west drainage. Later, after arriving at the fire line construction site, Mackey radioed IC Blanco that the fire had crossed the fire line and was burning actively. Mackey's crew began building a line from H-1 down the east side of the fire.

July 6: Around 0030 hours, the jumper firefighters halted their work due to poor footing and falling rock. In smokejumper Kevin Erickson's narrative, he explains this part of their dangerous work: "We went to the helispot and decided to cut down off the east side at night. We followed the fire edge and after working for a while we decided to head back up to the top. We were working down in chutes. It was steep, with rolling rocks and dangerous at night. We tried cup trenching but could not hold the line." They returned to H-1. At 0300, they reported that the fire was burning actively on the ridgeline with ten-mile-per-hour winds blowing from the east.

Before daylight, at 0430, eleven of the BLM/Forest Service firefighters began their long arduous hike back to the fire, choosing an east drainage route that differed from the previous day's route. Anticipating staying overnight, they carried extra saws, gas, food, and water.

Around 0530, Don Mackey contacted the dispatch office and requested a helicopter with a longline to sling their gear from the jump site down to the helispot. At this time, he also reported that the fire had grown in size. His plan was to finish the fire line from H-1 north along the ridge and then gather the jump gear.

About an hour later, the Prineville, Oregon, Hotshot Crew was assigned to the fire. The hotshots are firefighters used for direct attack on active wildfires. These teams are normally made up of twenty firefighters including a firefighter superintendent. They use a variety of hand tools and chainsaws and work with water/retardant-dropping aircraft when needed.

A few days earlier, the hotshots had been battling a wildfire in central Oregon. They were released from that incident after helping to bring the fire under control.

The state of Colorado, with its rising temperatures, lack of moisture, and outbreak of dozens of fires, was in dire need of additional firefighters. After being released from the Oregon fire, the Prineville crew were transported to the airfield at Klamath Falls, Oregon, where they boarded a chartered aircraft and departed for Grand Junction, Colorado. Ironically, they would soon overtake and pass a cold front moving eastward. One day later, the Prineville Hotshots and that same cold front would meet head-on in a deadly battle, a battle that would end tragically for some of those firefighters, on Storm King Mountain.

The helicopter that had been ordered earlier by smokejumper Mackey was dispatched from Grand Junction. On board the Aerospatiale helicopter, registration number 93R, was Richard Good (pilot), Steve Little, Robert Browning, and Rich Tyler, all members of the helitack crew.

Good had earned his wings and helicopter training through the US Army's Rotary Wing Flight Training program. Like most graduating helicopter pilots at the time, Good was sent to South Vietnam, chalking up hundreds of flight hours flying combat missions during that Southeast Asian war. The flying he was about to face, working on the South Canyon Fire, would challenge even this battle-hardened pilot's experience and limitations.

The helicopter would be operating out of a temporary helibase, located at Canyon Creek Estates, only a few miles west of the active fire. Before this day ended, Good's flying would consist of shuttling firefighters from the helibase to Helispot 2, water bucket drops, reconnaissance flights, and ultimately, search, rescue, and recovery missions.

CHAPTER TWELVE

Reinforcements and Battling the Fire

At 09:30, the helicopter arrived at the fire and landed at Helispot 2. The first flight for 93R would be a reconnaissance flight with Blanco, Mackey, Browning, Tyler, and pilot Good on board. During the recon, Mackey directed the smokejumpers on the ground to begin building a fire line downhill. After discussing strategy and making sketches of the active fire, Blanco, Mackey, and the two helitack crewmen were dropped off at Helispot 2.

Around 10:30, a second smokejumper aircraft, Jumper 17, arrived over the fire with eight jumpers on board. They parachuted safely into the jump site, winds being light at zero to five miles per hour at this time. Dale Longanecker is the designated jumper-in-charge of this group of jumpers. After contact with Mackey, Longanecker's jumpers were directed to start down the west flank of the fire, building a direct line. Their fire line was six to seven feet wide as they worked downhill.

At noon on July 6, the Prineville Hotshots arrived at the helibase by bus. By 12:30, ten of the Hotshot Crew were ferried by helicopter 93R into Helispot 2. Normally, the hotshot crews work as a team and very seldom split into different work groups. With only one helicopter working on the fire, pilot Good was tasked with ferrying the firefighters to H-2, making water drops, and moving cargo by sling load.

The Prineville Hotshot Superintendent Tom Shepard had flown in as part of the first ten hotshots to arrive at Helispot 2. There, Shepard, Blanco, and Mackey discussed firefighting strategy and agreed to send the first nine hotshots down to help the jumpers working on the west flank fire line. Mackey proceeded down the line to rejoin the jumpers and the nine hotshots. Blanco and Shepard departed Helispot 2, hiking to the original Helispot 1 to further discuss tactics and strategy while awaiting the arrival of the other ten hotshots.

At 13:00, the fire flared up on the west flank. Good was called to make water bucket drops. The ground crews had considered retreating but stayed on-site after the water drops were effective in cooling and controlling the flare-up. At the time of the flare-up, the anticipated cold front arrived in Grand Junction. The South Canyon firefighters have only two hours and twenty minutes before the battle for their very existence begins.

After completing about a dozen water drops, Good returned to the helibase and began ferrying the remaining ten Prineville Hotshots into H-2, where they began improving and helping to hold the line along the ridge between H-2 and H-1. There were also thirty more smokejumpers en route to the helibase by bus, to be transported to the fire later.

Around 14:00, the smokejumpers and hotshots took a lunch break on the southwest corner of the fire, to be referenced as the "lunch spot" later in the accident investigation. For one smokejumper, the lunch spot would be the key to his survival.

After the thirty-minute lunchbreak, the firefighters continued working and improving the fire line. Longanecker headed downhill to the south from the lunch spot to scout out some of the spot fires. About this same time, firefighters at the helibase observed and reported that the fire activity was increasing west of Helispot 1. As forecast and predicted, the cold front had now arrived at the fire.

In his statement, Longanecker described what he found after leaving the lunch spot and the other firefighters:

I left the group. I told them it was a relatively safe area if the fire blew up. I told Petrilli that I was going to check it out. I got to the first area of active burning. It was small. I called Tony to tell him to send a chainsaw but first I would get a bucket drop. I got one drop and then the fire activity picked up on top so they asked for the bucket and gave it to them. After I lost the bucket I told Tony to stay out in the wash until we got the bucket back. I stayed near the active area, which was a fair shag from the bottom—200 yards. When I was checking out the spot I was in a bad location to see what was happening. Tony was out in the open wash and could see. I did notice some torching in the interior. At that time the helicopter pilot said the activity was picking up and shortly after that Tony told us that it had spotted across the canyon. I knew that I needed to get to the safety zone. I could see in the bottom that it had crossed the canyon and burning at a high rate of speed.

On top, the fire had spotted across the ridgetop fire line. Blanco directed Ryerson and Scholz to scout the ridgeline. They reported that the spot fires had crossed the line and called for the helicopter to make water drops. Blanco called dispatch and notified them that the fire and wind activity had increased.

CHAPTER THIRTEEN

Blowup, Entrapment, and Escape

At 1600 hours, the fire crossed the west drainage at the base of the gully, below Longanecker's location. Earlier, Longanecker had contacted

The fire blowup that occurred between 4:30 and 5:00 p.m. PHOTOGRAPH COURTESY OF THE US FOREST SERVICE.

Tony Petrilli to have a saw and a couple of diggers to come down to his location.

Petrilli describes this part in his statement: "Thomas, Shelton, who had the other radio in our group, and I started down. We walked 10 yards and stopped. The fire made a run in the crowns up the hill from Longanecker. We were impressed with the 100-foot flame lengths and the radiant heat we were feeling even though the fire was 250–300 yards away. What was even more impressive was that the ground fuel was already burnt from earlier during the fire. The fire would travel 150 yards in fifteen seconds."

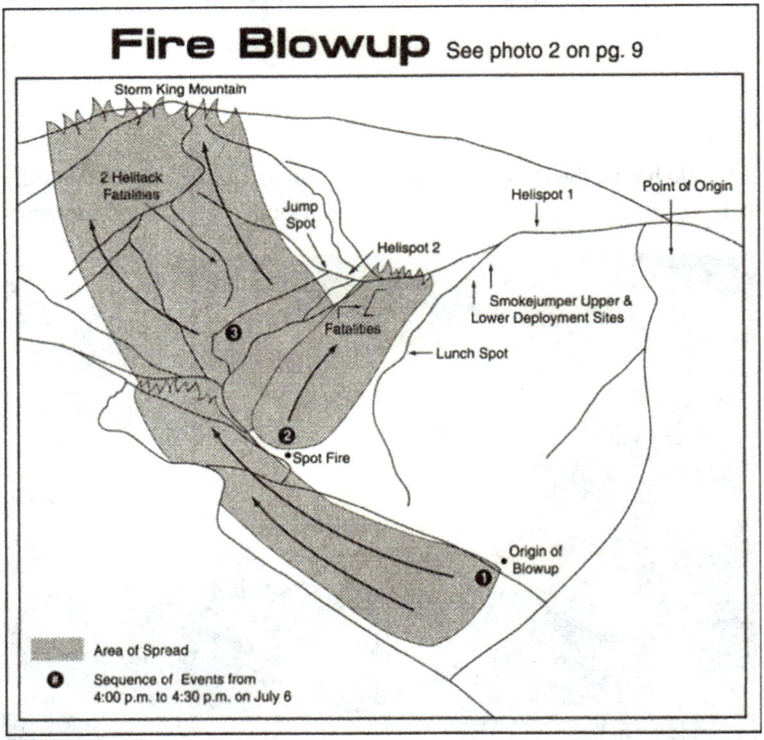

Drawing of the fire blowup. COURTESY OF THE US FOREST SERVICE.

Petrilli continues his description of the fire crossing the main canyon:

> *At approx. 1600–1605 it spotted across the main canyon. I called Mackey on the radio and told him it had spotted across the main canyon and that we were coming back up the hill. I knew I didn't want to be where I was. He asked me if it spotted across the MAIN canyon. I replied yes it was across the main canyon and it's ROLLING. At this time its flame front was 50 yards wide and had traveled 50 yards from when we first noticed it as a spot. It was definitely pushed by high winds, approx. 35 mph. This was a very narrow spot in the canyon where the winds were also being funneled.*
>
> *As we were coming up to the lunch spot Mackey met us and we all agreed that the place to go would be in the black up the ridge from the lunch spot and below H-1. The one place I knew I didn't want to go was back down the line. To the right was the gulley that Longanecker was in. The area where we were didn't look safe either. This is also where we met up again with Cooper and Feliciano. At this point the winds were approx. 45 mph. As we were going up I was at the tail to see if we had everyone. I thought Mackey was with us, but I didn't see him. I figured he was going back down the line to get everybody else. He didn't have to come to direct us, but he did. He didn't have to go back down the line to get everybody else, but he did.*

Appendix 4 of the investigative report's chronology describes the events between 1600 and 1624 hours. Each event is described separately for the four main groups of firefighters involved.

> *1. Jumpers That Deploy Their Fire Shelters Below Helispot*
>
> *Thomas and Petrilli notice that the fire is in the gulley and has crossed to the other side of the main drainage. At about 1610 the jumpers meet Mackey at the lunch spot. Mackey tells them to climb the hill and they will find a good burned safety area below Helispot 1. Petrilli calls Longanecker*

and tells him to get out of there into the burned area. They last see Mackey as he leaves to check on Longanecker. Mackey tells the other firefighters on the ridge to go to Helispot 1. The jumpers climb the hill to seek an adequate safety zone and to distance themselves from the blowup. The smoke jumpers drop their Sigg bottles and saws partway up the hill. Soto has leg cramps and falls behind. Woods stays back with Soto. Woods and Soto deploy their shelters between the upper group and the saws.

Petrilli describes this climb and the difficult conditions they were facing: "The steep slope, smoke, ash, and blowing dust were some of the difficult factors we had to deal with. Soto and Woods were dealing with muscle cramps and dehydration. The noise of the firestorm in the canyon was like a jet during take off. The wind was still at 45 mph. Soto and Woods began to fall behind. I passed them, but kept encouraging them to keep coming and ensuring them there was good black up the hill. The area we were going through was black, but the aerial fuels were still there. I didn't want to stay there because I just witnessed previously the hillside reburn with very high intensity. I still didn't know what was going on with the fire below us. There was still very heavy smoke coming from below."

Six other firefighters (Thomas, Petrilli, Cooper, Feliciano, Shelton, and Rhoades) move up just below Helispot 1 and have time to clear areas and remove their chainsaw chaps. They have difficulty deploying their fire shelters because of winds strong enough to blow their hard hats off. The smoke jumpers radio Mackey between 1619 and 1621 hours to report that they are in their shelters. They do not remember Mackey's reply. They remain in their shelters for about 1.5 hours until Longanecker arrives at the site. Longanecker waits out the fire near the lunch spot and does not deploy a shelter.

2. Group on Ridgeline

Half of the Prineville Hotshots, Ryerson's squad, and the two helitack crew members (Tyler and Browning) are on the ridgetop at this time. Byers is working the farthest up the line toward Helispot 1, and the hotshots are all working the spot fire or are nearby. Fire activity is increasing, with several spot fires. Ryerson calls in water drops. At 1604 Blanco gives the order to proceed to Helispot 1. They make it to the big rock just below the burned area when they receive the message that the way up is blocked, and they should turn around and go to Helispot 2. Archuleta waits just north of the point where the fireline ties into the ridge, until all the firefighters coming down from Helispot 1 pass him. He then follows them to Helispot 2. Everyone runs to the red packs, where Blanco and Shepard direct them down the east drainage. This is the last point of contact with Tyler and Browning, who from the ridgeline yell at everyone to go up the ridge. They are told to drop down into the drainage but choose not to.

3. Group on the West Flank

The hotshots and smoke jumpers are improving and holding the fireline between the lunch spot and the saddle. Doehring and Archuleta have already worked their way back up the hill with the chainsaw. Erickson arrives at the tree from the bottom and stops there with Haugh. Haugh and Erickson decide to stay until the crew is in view. As they are waiting, the fire becomes very active, and crews are directed to move out of the bottom. As the crew comes into view, the fire spots across the drainage to the east side below them in the bottom of the drainage. Erickson radios Mackey between 1614 and 1618 to tell him about the spot fire below him. Erickson takes a picture as the crew comes into view and flames roar over the spur ridge behind the firefighters. He puts his camera around his neck, and Haugh grabs him to go up the hill. From the ridgeline Doehring and Archuleta can see the last two firefighters in line. Reaching the tree where Erickson and Hough are standing, Thrash says to deploy shelters. Haugh turns and runs to the ridge, followed by Erickson. Haugh reports that the crew is walking briskly but is still in line, carrying equipment and apparently not aware of the closeness of the fire until Erickson radios Mackey that fire has spotted directly below them. Hipke says that they walked quickly when they went up the line until they got to the last steep pitch. Hipke does not deploy because of the density of the fuels. He runs around Roth and Thrash. About halfway up the last pitch, he sees Erickson and Haugh telling the firefighters to drop equipment and run. The rest of the crew is 20 to 30 yards behind Hipke. Hipke is running, while trying to remove his shelter from its case. A blast of hot air knocks Hipke to the ground. He thinks the main heat passes over him. Haugh described the main fire cresting the ridge with 200- to 300-foot flame lengths, 2 to 3 seconds after he bailed over the top. Hipke dives over the top of the ridge, and Haugh, Erickson, and Hipke run 200 to 300 feet and stop. Erickson and Haugh then attend to Hipke's burned hands. Doehring and Archuleta believe that 30 to 45 seconds elapse between when they take their photo and when the fire crests the ridge. Erickson believes that the spot fire moved from the bottom of the drainage to the top of the ridge in about 30 seconds.

Flames and smoke pictured on top of ridge. PHOTOGRAPH COURTESY OF THE US FOREST SERVICE.

The people that dropped off the ridge to the east take various routes down the drainage. The fire moves down to the mouth of the drainage about 30 to 40 minutes after the last person has escaped.

PHOTOGRAPHS COURTESY OF S. ARCHULETA AND S. DOEHRING.

Brad Hough described his race to outrun the fire:

There was a slight ridge behind the crew which obscured our view of the bottom of the fire. The crew was walking through Gambel oak approx. 7' tall. As best as I can re-collect the fire roared behind the ridge, and that was the first indication of how bad it had gotten. Jumper Thrash made it to our location at the tree and said should we deploy? I replied no we have to make it over the ridge. The firestorm literally exploded behind the ridge with approx. 100' flame height. At this point I decided I had to run. I can't recall if anyone was ahead of me or not, nor can I recall what the crew's reaction was to the blow-up. As I neared the crest of the ridge the heat was intense. I topped out and headed down the other side about 150' when I turned around a wall of flame 150' tall and 1/4 mile wide was on the ridge-top and starting to roll down the east side of the ridge. I ran approx. another 150' when I literally ran into Kevin Erickson. I am not sure if we spoke or not, but at the same time, Eric Hipke emerged from the brush with his hands badly burnt. Sensing real danger we opted to go lower on the ridge before we stopped to dress Eric's wounds. Using T-shirts, towels, and bandannas, we wrapped Hipke's hands and hurried him down the ridge to the drainage at the bottom. We hooked up with the other survivors and hiked out to the interstate.

4. Helitack Crew

The helitack crew (Tyler and Browning) were at Helispot 2 directing helicopter operations. They are last seen going up the hill from Helispot 2. Blanco and Shepard direct them down the east drainage, but they continue up the ridge out of sight, yelling, "Run the ridge." That is the last contact with them. Helicopter 93R pilot Good, attempts radio contact but receives no answer. Tyler and Browning run the ridge above the jump site. The fire

East drainage escape route. PHOTOGRAPH COURTESY OF THE US FOREST SERVICE.

funnels through the saddle at the jump site and cuts off a route to the east. The slope to the northwest looks relatively flat with rock outcrops. The route appears to be the best. Being flanked by the fire, Tyler and Browning head northwest. In 150–200 yards, they run into a steep 50-foot-deep rocky chute. Trying to cross the chute, they are caught by the fire in the bottom.

CHAPTER FOURTEEN

Aftermath

Tony Petrilli describes the last minutes of the disastrous events taking place while in his fire shelter:

When we were in our shelter I talked to Longanecker. He said he was on the ridge below us and that he was fine. I told him that we were OK. To keep spirits up we talked and joked. Ken Wabaunsee called us from the heli-base. Wabaunsee was in charge of a group of jumpers that had been bussed to the fire. They just arrived to see our fire shelters on the ridge. He had no idea what had happened. I told him that there were nine of us on the ridge and we were OK, but we didn't know what the fire was doing below us. Wabaunsee then told me that Erickson and Hipke made it to the highway and needed an ambulance to take them to the hospital. He then told us that Archuleta and Doehring made it to the freeway. We started getting a head count of all the jumpers. We were missing Mackey, Thrash, and Roth. I called them on the radio. No reply. I called them again. No reply. I remembered when Wabaunsee was talking to Erickson I couldn't hear Erickson's transmissions. I had hoped that Mackey and Roth were by the freeway and couldn't get radio transmissions in or out.

When in the shelters the fire made three different runs on our right side approx. 200 yards away. Inside the shelter it heated up to 110 degrees. During the hottest run there were glowing fire brands blowing into the shelter. Between fire runs we would peek out the shelter. The wind was still blowing ash and dust. There was still heavy smoke coming from below us. Inside the shelter there was much less ash, dust, and smoke.

At approx. 1730 an air tanker dropped a load in our area. At approx. 1800 Tanker 10 dropped a load that landed directly on us. Smoke from below was not as heavy, but the (retardant) gave us a little more reassurance. Soto and Woods carried their shelters closer to us. At approx. 1830 we decided to get out of our shelters. Longanecker came to our area. I asked him if he had to shelter up. He said that he hadn't and that where he was it was fine. We were trying to organize a sweep of the hillside to look for the missing. He said that he was going to the helispot.

As we were looking into the canyon we noticed something below the saddle on the line that didn't look like the surrounding area. Instead of sweeping I headed straight for that area. I walked straight to the lower group of bodies. I called the helicopter and said that I had found five. He asked if we needed medi-vac. I told him that it was too late for that. I walked up the hill and found six more. Called the helicopter again and informed them of the additional six. After I found the twelfth body I walked over to the helispot.

The two helitack crewmen were found a short time later, bringing the number of fatalities to fourteen.

Unless noted otherwise, all photos, illustrations, and sketches are from the official South Canyon Fire investigation dated August 17, 1994.

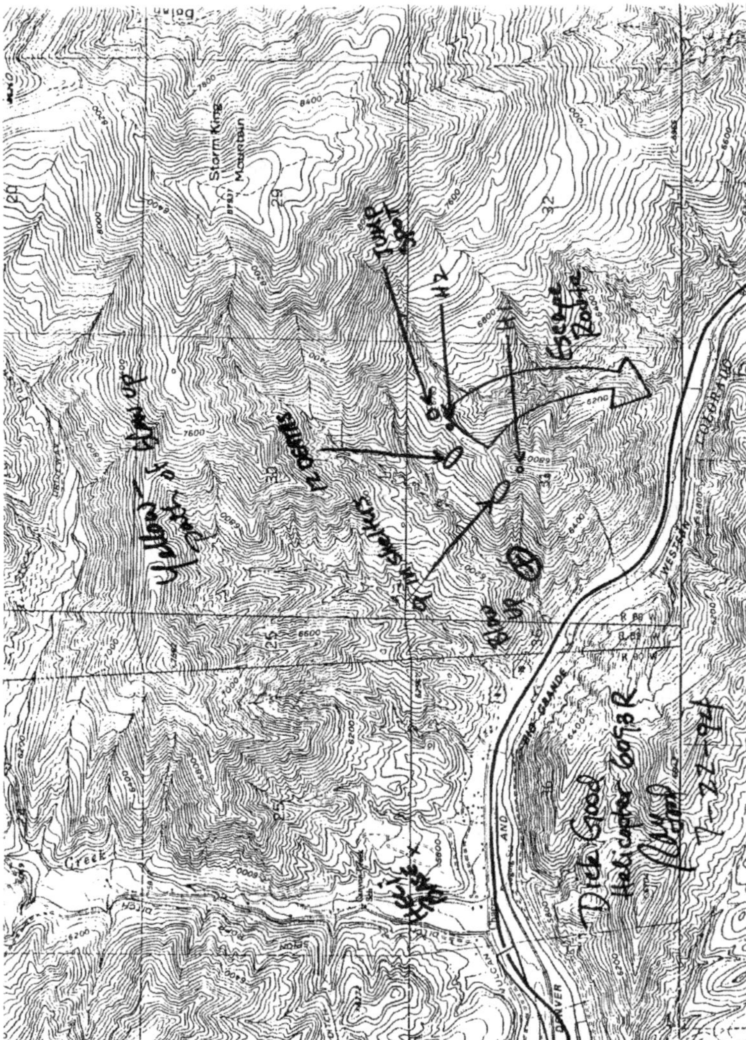

Pilot Good's sketch of the fire aftermath. COURTESY OF THE US FOREST SERVICE.

CHAPTER FIFTEEN

Conclusion and Findings

The investigation into the fire and tragic loss of life began immediately. Over the course of the investigation, several factors were cited as contributing to the disastrous loss of life and injuries to the firefighters.

The Prineville Hotshots had not been thoroughly briefed on the fire. They were not familiar with the type of fuels they were dealing with or the weather conditions they would face. Most of the firefighters were unaware of the Red Flag Warnings. One factor in the investigation report states: "The fire behavior on July 6 could have been predicted on the basis of fuels, weather, and topography, but fire behavior information was not requested or provided. Therefore, critical information was not available for developing strategy and tactics."

Helicopter 93R, because of a state law, was not authorized to dip water out of the river, which was close by and would have allowed quicker turnarounds for water drops on the fire. The law restricting sling loads across highways has since been rescinded in Colorado.

Many of the firefighters were not sure who oversaw the fire, causing some confusion during work assignments. Inadequate safety zones and escape routes were also contributing factors.

Investigation Conclusion:

Firefighters and fire managers are engaged in a complex business with inherent risks, which requires skill, good judgment, and the ability to make difficult decisions. The South Canyon fire tragedy resulted from a series of judgments, decisions, events, and actions with serious cumulative impacts.

No one person or unit recognized the interaction of all factors on the incident that resulted in the entrapments. Firefighting safety fundamentals were compromised during a period of extreme weather and fire behavior in a highly flammable fuel type. This situation, compounded by failure to provide critical fire weather and fire behavior information to the firefighters, was the primary cause of the injuries and fatalities.

In Memory of the South Canyon Fire Firefighters:

Kathi W. Beck
Tamera J. Bickett
Scott A. Blecha
Levi Brinkley
Robert E. Browning, Jr.
Douglas M. Dunbar
Teri A. Hagen
Don M. Mackey
Bonnie J. Holtby
Jon R. Kelso
Jim Thrash
Rob Johnson
Roger Roth
Richard K. Tyler

CHAPTER SIXTEEN

High Desert Inferno

Destructive wildfires are commonly associated with destroying large swaths of forests while threatening lives and structures in their paths. Desert fires are frequent occurrences during the hot, dry summer months, but in most cases, they are not a major threat to lives and property. They can usually be extinguished rather quickly and safely.

During the late evening hours on July 28, 1995, a desert fire southeast of the small town of Kuna, Idaho, would prove how deadly and out of control a desert fire can be when several unexpected circumstances and events combined, turning a small controllable fire into a deadly inferno.

Kuna is in southwest Idaho, on what is known as the Snake River Plain. The town was established as a result of an east–west railroad line being built through the area in the early 1880s. In 1882, a construction camp was set up where the railroad line intersected a stagecoach trail and way station, known as Fifteen Mile Station. After the railroad line was completed, a railway station was established at that same location, and the name changed to Kuna. The stagecoach line stretched for seventy-two miles from Boise City to the booming mining camp of Silver City. The entire area was considered a high desert. Today, Kuna is part of the explosive growth affecting the southwestern part of Idaho known as the Treasure Valley. Many of the cities within the Treasure Valley border the high desert.

Fire protection for Kuna is provided by the Kuna Rural Fire District. It covers Kuna and the surrounding areas. The firefighters are trained in battling structure fires, providing emergency medical services, and fighting wildfires.

On July 27, 1995, and on the following morning, the National Weather Service in Boise issued a forecast and warning for the possibility of gusty, erratic winds up to fifty-five miles per hour near any thunderstorms. At noon on July 28, the National Weather Service issued a Fire Weather Watch for dry lightning and a forecast of thunderstorms moving through western Idaho in the late afternoon and evening.

Early spring had brought a higher amount of moisture than normal to that area, resulting in an unusual amount of cheatgrass growth. The sagebrush was also dense and mature. As summer approached, temperatures began to climb, reaching the upper nineties in July. The fuels became tinder dry.

At 6:29 p.m., Danskin Peak Lookout reported a lightning-sparked fire approximately sixteen miles southwest of Boise. Several citizens and the Ada County Dispatch also reported the fire.

Within minutes of the reported fire, the Bureau of Land Management's Boise District Dispatch Center launched a firefighting unit with two Type 4X wildland fire engine vehicles and a Type 6X slip-on firetruck. The unit, known as the "Wild West Unit," arrived at the fire at around 1900 hours.

As the fire grew in size and intensity, several more BLM firetrucks and a water tender were dispatched, along with a transport truck carrying a bulldozer. Dave Kerby, the crew boss for the Wild West Unit, was designated as the Incident Commander in charge of the overall firefighting operation.

When the Wild West Unit first arrived at the scene, the fire was estimated at sixty to sixty-five acres with winds from the west at four to six miles per hour. Flame lengths along the flanks of the fire were three to five feet, actively burning in dense cheatgrass and three- to four-foot-tall sagebrush.

A BLM helicopter was dispatched to the fire and picked up Kerby for an aerial reconnaissance of the fire. The Boise BLM Dispatch radioed IC Kerby and asked if the Kuna Rural Fire District (Kuna RFD) was on scene. Kerby responded that he had not seen any equipment or personnel from the RFD. Shortly after landing from his helicopter tour, Kuna Fire Chief Rich Cromwell (Kuna 650) contacted Kerby and asked if assistance was needed. IC Kerby replied that he could use a brush truck and a water tender.

At 1907, Kuna Fire Chief Cromwell radioed Kuna RFD Captain Doyle McPherson and told him to respond to the Point Fire with two brush trucks and a water tender. Captain McPherson was put in charge of the Kuna firefighters and was instructed by Cromwell to keep the two brush trucks together. Kuna Engine 620, a 1,500-gallon brush truck; Kuna Engine 622, a 1,750-gallon brush truck; and Kuna Engine 625, a 2,500-gallon water tender would be responding to the fire.

Like most rural, volunteer fire departments, Kuna RFD relies on available firefighters, volunteers from all walks of life that may have the day off from their regular jobs, or qualified volunteers that can delay or drop what they are doing and respond quickly to a fire call.

Kuna RFD's normal assignment policy was two firefighters per vehicle. Each driver had to be qualified to operate the truck and equipment. Firefighters were not assigned to certain trucks. Pairing of firefighters was random and relied on the first two personnel that arrived, provided at least one firefighter was a qualified driver.

William Buttram and Joshua Oliver arrived at the fire station and assumed command of brush truck 620. Buttram was qualified as the driver.

Buttrum started as a volunteer firefighter with the Kuna RFD in October 1994. This was nine months prior to the Point Fire. Wildfire season for the area usually goes from May through September, so Buttram had very little wildland firefighting experience prior to the Point Fire. The 1995 season would be his first wildfire season. William

Buttram was thirty-one years old and a full-time employee of the Idaho Department of Corrections, working as a prison guard.

Joshua Oliver also became a volunteer firefighter for the Kuna Rural Fire Department in October of 1994. The 1995 wildland fire season would be his first season fighting wildfires also. Oliver was eighteen years old and had not yet qualified as a firetruck driver.

Engine 620 left the fire station around 1911 hours with Buttrum as the driver, Oliver in the front passenger seat, and Captain McPherson as a back seat passenger.

Responding to the fire in brush truck 622 were volunteer firefighters Michael Law and Robert Black. Both firefighters were experienced; Law had worked as a volunteer firefighter since 1976, and Black since 1970. Water tender 625 was crewed by Captain Joseph Stear and Jenny Taylor. Captain Stear had more than a decade of firefighting experience; Taylor had very little.

Arriving at the Point Fire around 7:30 p.m., at a location just up the road from the northeast perimeter of the fire and bordering Swan Falls Road, the three Kuna vehicle crews met for a briefing given by Captain McPherson. During the briefing, McPherson again repeated Chief Cromwell's instructions: brush trucks 620 and 622 were to stay together, and all Kuna personnel were to take orders from the BLM Incident Commander and to maintain radio contact with the BLM crews on the fire. The crews were also told to switch to the BLM radio channel 16, to stay in safe zones, to get into the black burned-out areas in case of any trouble, and to be aware of escape routes.

At the conclusion of the briefing, Captain McPherson instructed the 620 and 622 crews to join up with the BLM Incident Commander for their assignments. McPherson had decided to stay with 625, the water tender truck. Shortly after the brush trucks had departed, Captain McPherson discovered that the radio in the water tender was not capable of monitoring or transmitting on the BLM's channel 16. He would only be able to monitor and transmit on the Kuna radio channel. Back at the Kuna Fire Station, after leaving his vehicle that did have the

BLM channel 16 capability, Chief Cromwell could only monitor and transmit on the Kuna station's radio frequency also. Communications would become a major factor in the unfolding events yet to come.

Under Findings of Fact, stated in a civil court case proceedings over this tragic accident, item numbers 40, 41, and 42 describe the significance of the radio frequencies and the serious effect it would have on communications between the fire bosses and the fire truck occupants.

FINDINGS OF FACT

40. *The radios on 620 and 622 had a scan capability. When set in a scan mode, the radios automatically switched between BLM's channel 16 and the Kuna frequency, broadcasting whatever messages cane over those channels, and allowing the occupants of the trucks to monitor both channels without having to manually operate the radio. If both channels were broadcasting at the same time, the Kuna frequency would 'step on' BLM's channel 16, so that only the Kuna broadcast could be heard.*

41. *If the radios were not set on scan mode, the occupants could only hear the single frequency that they had manually chosen.*

42. *As 620 and 622 pulled away from the initial staging area, Captain Stear (driver of water tender truck 625) noticed that 620 had some loose gear on the back of the truck. He tried to reach 620 on the Kuna channel but 620 did not respond. This is some evidence that 620's radio was either not working properly or that 620 had manually selected the BLM channel, and had not put its radio on scan mode.*

Proceeding south on Swan Falls Road, 620 and 622 arrived at the northeast corner of the fire. The Kuna RFD crews contacted IC Kerby on the BLM channel 16 and requested assignments for the Kuna vehicles. Kerby instructed the two Kuna brush trucks to fall in behind BLM truck Engine 61 and to work the northern perimeter. Another

BLM truck, Engine 83, would follow behind the Kuna trucks. The four trucks were assigned to directly attack the northern flank of the fire, starting from Swan Falls Road and working westward around the fire's perimeter. BLM Engine 09 was sent to directly attack the southern flank, working west from Swan Falls Road. Kuna 625 water tender was to go south on Swan Falls Road to the southeast corner of the fire and standby for refilling operations.

Applying water through the front bumper nozzles, 620 and 622 had an immediate effect, diminishing the flames and causing a change in smoke color, indicating fire suppression.

After the BLM and Kuna trucks had traveled approximately a quarter mile in the westerly direction, IC Kerby radioed Kuna 622 to move in closer to the perimeter and to proceed around the entire perimeter of the fire. Kuna 620 and 622 complied, and in tandem, drove around the BLM engines. Engine 620 began working on a flare-up on the fire line using the same suppression method, spraying the fire as they drove alongside the burning grass and sagebrush. Firetruck 622 followed 620, but now conserving their water.

At 8:10 p.m., with the fire engines working both flanks of the fire, the southern flank vehicles, traveling in a clockwise manner, and the northern flank trucks, moving counterclockwise around the perimeter, met up and successfully stopped the spread of the fire. The size of the fire at that time was estimated at one hundred twenty acres.

After passing BLM engines 425 and 09 and the dozer that was cutting a fire line on the southern perimeter, Kuna 620 and 622 continued mopping up along the southern flank, and heading east, ended up at the southeast corner of the fire and Swan Falls Road.

After completing the trip around the fire, the Kuna crews then asked for further instructions. IC Kerby instructed the brush truck crews to turn around and work back around the fire's perimeter, soaking it down as they went. Engines 620 and 622 complied and began working the southern flank in a westerly direction, with Kuna 622 in the lead this time.

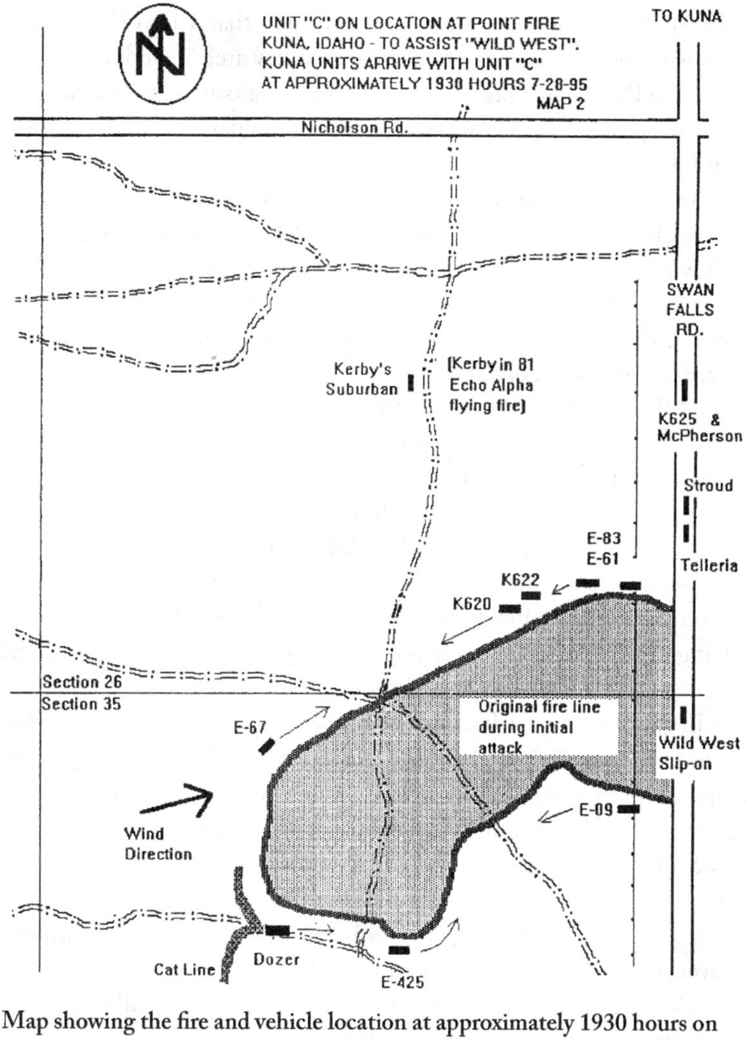

Map showing the fire and vehicle location at approximately 1930 hours on July 28. COURTESY OF THE US DEPARTMENT OF THE INTERIOR AND BUREAU OF LAND MANAGEMENT.

A little after 8:15 p.m., the National Weather Service called the Boise BLM dispatch office and notified them that a Red Flag Warning was being issued for the Snake River Valley area, including the area where the Point Fire was burning. The warning contained information about an approaching thunderstorm with accompanying winds of more than fifty miles per hour.

At 8:22 p.m., the BLM dispatch called IC Kerby over the BLM channel 16, notifying him of the Red Flag Warning and the impending high winds. Since the Red Flag Warning was transmitted by the BLM dispatch office over their channel 16 radio, Kerby felt that all firefighters working the Point Fire had heard the alert, and there was no need to ensure that everyone had heard it.

At the time IC Kerby was receiving the Red Flag Warning, Kuna 622 and 620 were on the southern perimeter moving west and about a quarter mile away from the point where they had turned around.

It was unclear whether 620 had heard the Red Flag Warning over the channel 16 frequency. Kuna Fire Department's radio channel transcript shows that at 8:24 p.m., Buttram had radioed Captain McPherson on the Kuna channel and asked about allowing Josh to get some driving time in since they were just doing mop-up and tucked in behind 622. Captain McPherson denied the request.

In the Findings of Fact, the timing of the radio transmissions was of concern. If the BLM channel 16 logbook and the Kuna radio transcripts were precise, then just two minutes after the red flag message was transmitted on the BLM channel 16, Buttram had contacted Captain McPherson on the Kuna frequency. This could indicate that Buttram and Oliver may have heard the Red Flag Warning and decided to contact McPherson about giving Josh Oliver the driving time anyway. However, if the times recorded on the call logs were off by a minute or two, it's possible that Bill Buttram was making his radio call to Captain McPherson at the same time the Red Flag Warning was being transmitted, causing Buttrum and Oliver to miss the warning.

BLM and Kuna fire engines working the Point Fire. PHOTOGRAPH COURTESY OF THE BUREAU OF LAND MANAGEMENT.

After the Red Flag Warning was broadcast at 8:22 p.m., and upon reaching the southwest corner of the fire, the brush trucks turned north, still soaking the perimeter's western flank. While working in tandem at the edge of the fire's perimeter, Kuna 622 ran out of water. Kuna volunteer Black radioed IC Kerby on the BLM channel 16 and told him they were out of water and asked for further instructions. Kerby instructed Black to travel to the water tender, refill, and then standby because a windstorm was about to pass through.

Engine 622 left the western perimeter and headed east through the already burned and blackened area toward Swan Falls Road. They then turned north just before reaching the eastern perimeter to find the opening in the fence that would allow them access to the road.

Just prior to reaching the fence opening and Swan Falls Road, Kuna 622 was contacted by 620 on the BLM radio channel and told them that their vehicle was overheating and they needed assistance. It didn't appear that the 620 crew was in any distress at this time. Engine 622 radioed back and told the 620 crew to remove the screen from in front of the radiator. It was not uncommon for the radiator screens to become clogged with debris, disrupting the airflow to the radiator while the trucks traveled through the dense grass and brush. Engine 620 acknowledged the instructions by replying, "Removing the screen."

At the time of 622's departure from the fire line, some confusion over Kuna 620's movements and intentions were brought up in testimony during litigation. Kuna firefighter Michael Law, the other crewman with Robert Black in 622, testified that immediately after IC Kerby had told them to go refill and standby, Kuna 620 radioed that they still had water and would stay on the line. However, Black was under the impression that 620 was empty also and would be following 622 in to refill. Captain Stear, in charge of the Kuna water tender 625, testified that when 622 arrived at the refill site, just down the road from the southeast corner of the fire, Black told him that 620 was behind them and would be refilling also. Because Stear's corroboration of Black's account of 620's intentions, the court favored Black's recollection of the event.

Sometime later, after 622 departed for refilling their water tank, 620 was observed on the west end where it passed BLM engines E-61 and E-67. Moving clockwise along the fire perimeter, 620 arrived at a two-track road running north–south where it intersected the fire line. For unknown reasons, Kuna 620 turned north on the two-track road where it then proceeded 1,945 feet, where it then drove east and then north–northeast cross-country through heavy sagebrush for another third of a mile. At this point, the Kuna RFD brush truck became disabled.

Back at the refilling site where brush truck 622 and water tender 625 waited, Captain McPherson started walking north on Swan Falls Road. About the middle of the east side perimeter, McPherson spotted the truck about 600 feet away in the burned-out area, heading in his direction and apparently with the intention of going to the fence opening on the northeast corner of the fire. McPherson started walking toward the fence opening with the intent of meeting up with 620's crew.

About this time, winds from the south increased dramatically. Stirring up the black ash and dust, visibility was soon reduced to zero. McPherson could hear 620 moving north at a high rate of speed.

Around 8:46 p.m., the fire, having been contained, blew up with the winds now gusting over forty miles an hour. Jumping the original fire line in several locations, the fire barreled northward at a frenzied pace. Flame lengths were estimated at twenty feet or more, with boiling smoke billowing out ahead of the raging wall of fire. The rate of spread was estimated at 560 feet per minute. From the fire's point of escape, it took only four minutes to overrun the stranded truck.

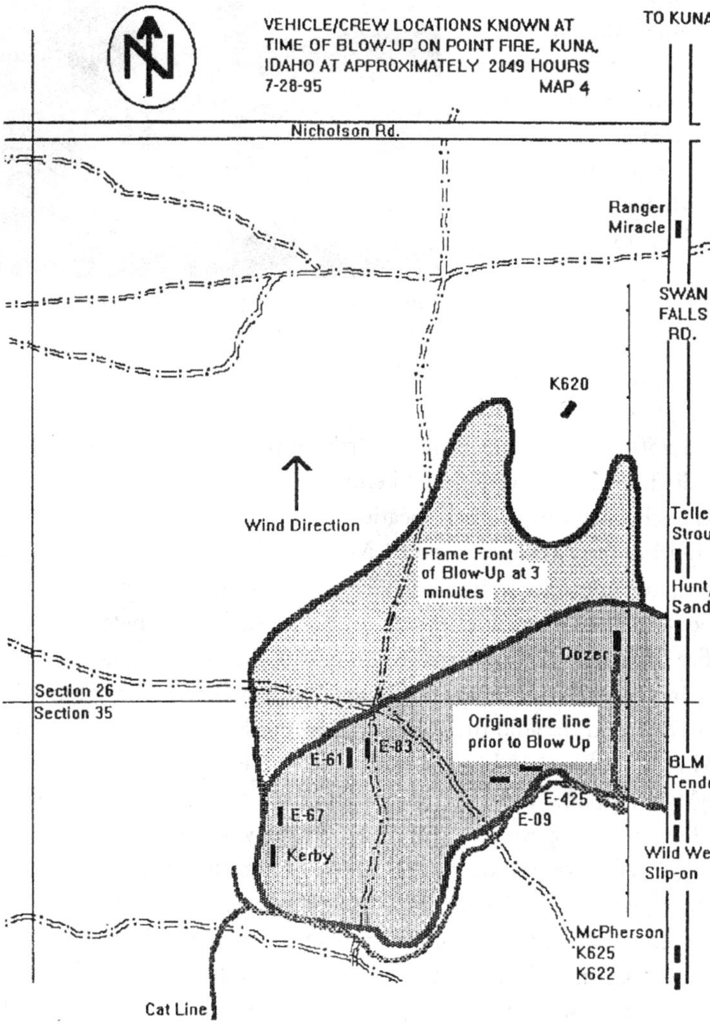

Map drawing of vehicle/crew locations at 2049 hours. COURTESY OF THE US DEPARTMENT OF THE INTERIOR AND BUREAU OF LAND MANAGEMENT.

Fire blowup at 8:46 p.m. PHOTOGRAPH COURTESY OF THE BUREAU OF LAND MANAGEMENT.

The Findings of Fact determined that the crew in Kuna 620 were trying to outrun the raging fire after missing the break in the fence that would have allowed them to escape onto the Swan Falls Road. Due to the obscured visibility, disorientation, and panic, they drove into heavy unburned sagebrush and high cheatgrass, traveling 1,750 feet from the original northern perimeter, where the truck then died. Heavy unburned fuel behind them exploded with fury and raced unchecked toward their location.

During the blowup, several BLM personnel, including a BLM fire investigator in a vehicle, immediately drove north on Swan Falls Road to about 2,000 feet beyond the original northern fire perimeter to assess the fire behavior. To their surprise and horror, they saw the stalled Kuna truck in the path of the approaching firestorm. They desperately and repeatedly tried to radio the Kuna Engine and Kuna Command on the BLM radio channel 16 but received no response.

At 8:49 p.m., Buttram, in the disabled truck, radioed Captain McPherson on the Kuna Command frequency and reported a frantic message: "We're on the north line, Doyle, we got fire coming hard and this thing has died." Captain McPherson answered the call, and Buttram then responded, "It's not going to let us out of here!"

Chief Cromwell then radioed Buttram and asked him to identify the problem. Buttram responded, "We're surrounded by fire!" Asked to repeat his message, Buttram stated, "The truck's been overtaken by fire!" That was the last communication that anyone had with the 620 crew.

From the Kuna RFD call log, recorded on tape, and as shown in the BLM investigation report, the final communications between Unit 620 (Buttram), Unit 6803 (Captain McPherson), and Unit 650 (Chief Cromwell) were as follows:

Buttram: Doyle, Buttram.

Unit 6803: 6803.

Buttram: We're on the north line, Doyle, we got fire coming hard, this thing has died.

Unit 6803: Is it on the [radio transmission cutting out]?

Buttram: Affirm. 6803, 6809. —it's not going to let us out of here.

Unit 650: 6803, 650.

Unit 650: 620, 650.

Buttram: Go ahead.

Unit 650: What kind of problem do you have?

Buttram: We're surrounded by fire.

Unit 650: Repeat?

Buttram: The truck has been overtaken by fire.

Unit 6803: Copy, we're en route.

This was the final radio contact with Buttram.

From the time that the Red Flag Warning was issued over the BLM radio frequency 16 at 8:22 p.m. and when the high winds hit the fire, only twenty-five minutes had elapsed. The thunderstorm had unleashed a monster.

After the passage of the flaming front, several attempts at rescue were made. Because of the intensity and ferocity of the fire still burning in the heavy fuels, rescue efforts by the Kuna and BLM crews were frustratingly hampered.

The call log, recorded on tape, describes communications between various units in the rescue effort as the out-of-control fire continued raging and expanding:

Unit 650: 620, 650. 620, 650. 625, 650. (Chief Cromwell trying to contact brush truck 620. When there is no answer, he then radios tanker 625.)

Unit 625: 25, go.

Unit 650: Give us approximate location of 620, where they're in trouble at?

Unit 625: I don't know they couldn't advise.

Unit 650: Copy. What side of the flank were they on?

Unit 625: Did you get in to—get in contact with 622, they were with them last.

Unit 650: Copy. 622, 650. (Other radio traffic caused a pause in 650's call.)

...

Unit 650: 622, 650.

Unit 641: 650, 641. I think Buttram said he was on the north flank.

Unit 650: Copy. 622, 650. Where's your location at?

Unit 622: We're west of Watt.

...

Unit 650: Calm down and talk slower so we can hear you. Repeat it. 622, repeat, but talk slower.

...

Unit 650: 641, did you copy that?

Unit 641: Copy.

...

Unit 625: 650, 625. One of the BLM trucks down here said they saw one of our trucks, just before the big wind, on the southwest corner of the fire.

Unit 650: Copy. We're headed to the northwest corner of the fire at this point.

At this time in the radio transcript, it shows that the radio transmissions between the units, dispatchers, and others became quite heavy due to requests for additional fire trucks from surrounding communities, police department aid for traffic control, medical personnel, and notification for Life Flight to stand by.

The raging fire continued unchecked, now threatening homes and other structures. It had jumped to the east side of Swan Falls Road and crossed to the north side of Nicolson Road.

The portions of the radio transmissions involving the search and rescue continue:

Unit 650: Unknown at this time until we get to our trucks, we are not sure if we have personnel that are burnt or not, if that's your reasoning for Life Flight.

Dispatch: Affirmative, 49 is putting them on standby.

Unit 650: 622, 650.

Unit 622: (Inaudible.)

Unit 650: Northbound on Swan Falls Road? How about 620? Where are they at? Copy?

Unknown: (Inaudible.)

Unit 622: At this point we are on the northwest section of the fire, heading towards it. We'll see if we cannot get through and get in to them.

Unit 650: Copy.

. . .

Unit 6803: 50, it's building pretty fast behind us, you might want to hit the road and get out.

. . .

Unit 650: We cannot get through to the northwest section of this thing, it's moving this way at about 20, 25 mile an hour at this point.

. . .

Unit 622: Doyle, this is 622. We cleared—we ran into a desperate situation here where we tried to get through the northern eastern flank and we were held up by fire, and so far, we haven't located those guys. Over.

Hey, also, Doyle, advise our incoming units that this is a very dangerous situation on the highway, to maybe back off. Because otherwise, they're going to get enveloped.

...

Unit 6803: Okay, do you have an injured subject somewhere. Medic 51 is here on location.

Unit 650: That's unknown at this time, 51, we have two guys who are missing. We are unable to locate at this time. Have them standby.

...

Unit 6803: 622, command.

Unit 622: This is 622.

Unit 6803: I want you to pull off and come back and go to our truck out in the brush.

Unit 622: Come back to you?

Unit 6803: Affirmative.

Unit 622: Coming back.

...

Unit 6803: Go ahead.

Unit 641: We've got a BLM engine up here, we're going to go ahead, as soon as we can, we're going to take off and go behind them and see if we can get in the black and go look for those guys.

Unit 650: Okay, we're right behind you.

Unit 641: We've located our men.

Unit 6803: Copy. Where are they at?

Unit 641: Still in the truck.

The intense, residual heat from the sagebrush made the first few attempts to reach Engine 620 all but impossible. At 9:21 p.m., the Kuna engine, brush truck 622, was finally able to approach 620. The truck was still engulfed in flames.

Engine 622 was able to extinguish the flames. The crew were then able to gain access to the truck. Tragically, William Buttram and Joshua Oliver had not survived the fire.

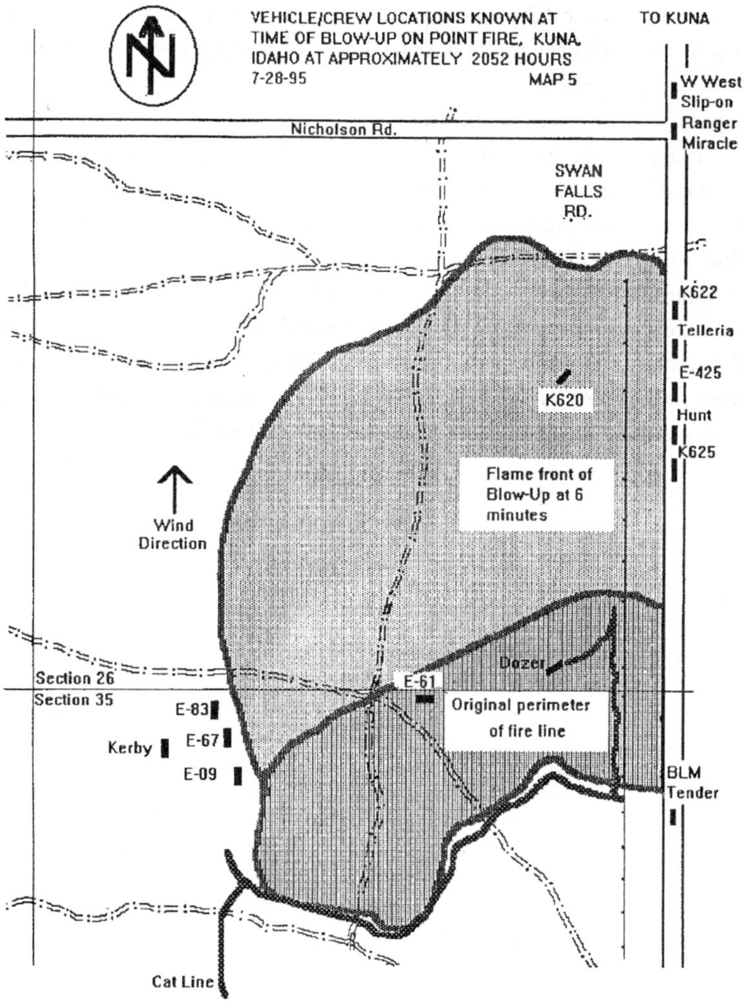

Map drawing of vehicle/crew location at 2052 hours. COURTESY OF THE US DEPARTMENT OF THE INTERIOR AND BUREAU OF LAND MANAGEMENT.

Rampage by Firestorm

Shortly after 620 was overrun, firefighters on Swan Falls Road observed a shift and an increase in the wind. Jumping the road, the fire made a rapid run to the northeast. It was estimated that 10,000 acres burned in the next three hours.

Fuels for the fire still consisted of the heavy sagebrush, cheatgrass, and now included grain fields. Fuels were interrupted in places by green fields, plowed fields, and roads. Despite this, the fire still burned for over nine miles. The rate of spread for the fast-moving fire was determined to be about 240 chains per hour (1 chain=66 feet).

Around midnight on July 28 the winds finally started subsiding. That day in 1995 had been devastating. Along with the loss of the two brave firefighters, 270 homes had to be evacuated, at least one home was destroyed, and several other structures were lost or damaged.

CHAPTER SEVENTEEN

Investigation and Findings

On July 31, 1995, the Bureau of Land Management convened a ten-member team comprising individuals from different government agencies. This team, led by Mike Green, who served as the District Manager with the Burns, Oregon, BLM, and Dan Friend, who was the Chief of Eagle Fire Protection District, was tasked with investigating the tragic loss of the two firefighters and the events leading up to the wildfire's devastating rampage.

As described in the accident report, the team's objective and charter was to:

1. *Identify factual data associated with the circumstances relating to the accident.*
2. *Accurately and objectively record the findings.*
3. *Analyze the findings to identify the significant factors involved and their relationships.*

4. *As appropriate, recommend actions that should be implemented immediately to prevent similar future occurrences.*
5. *Establish liaison with, and involve appropriately, local, county, state and federal officials who have a jurisdictional responsibility relative to this accident.*
6. *Develop and submit an investigation report as soon as possible, but no later than 45 days from the accident.*

The investigative team began their task by interviewing witnesses, visiting the accident site, and discussing the incident with Kuna Fire District members and BLM employees who had knowledge of and pertinent information vital to the investigation. Weather and burning conditions on the day of the accident were also very important factors in the investigation.

On July 29, the day after the burnover, Kuna RFD had the destroyed brush truck removed from the site and transported to a secure location. Prior to leaving the accident site, two mechanics inspected the truck's external drive train (shaft) for failure. No evidence was found to indicate any failure.

Communications

The investigation found that lack of common communications on the fire contributed to the incident. The BLM IC was unable to monitor Kuna Command because the Kuna frequency was not programmed into his radio. Some Kuna crews were able to communicate over both the BLM and Kuna frequencies, while others could not.

A critical lack of communications occurred when the crew of Kuna Engine 620 did not communicate their intentions when they left the fire line. The investigation also showed that the Salmon BLM crew (Engine 425), Kuna water tender 625, Kuna Command (6803), and the Ada County Dispatch Center did not hear the Red Flag Warning broadcast by the BLM Boise District Dispatch.

The report describes one critical summation of the fire's communications problem: "The problem with communication on the Point Fire was illustrated most dramatically at the time of the blowup. The Unit C Leader was aware of Kuna RFD Engine 620's location and the peril faced by the crew but could not contact anyone from Kuna. At the same time, Kuna Command knew of pending trouble, but did not know Engine 620's location, and was trying frantically to contact anyone who did."

Training and Complacency

When the investigators reviewed the training that the firefighters on the Point Fire had received, it consisted of a variety of experience and training for some. It ranged from years to just months.

BLM firefighter experience ranged from three months to twenty-nine seasons. Kuna RFD firefighters experience ranged from two months to twenty-one years.

The investigation report found that the Kuna firefighters were well trained for fighting structure fires, but the firefighters on the Point Fire only had five hours of wildland fire training in 1995. That training had been requested by the Kuna RFD in June and July of that year. The training was provided by the BLM Boise District.

The investigative team found that once the original fire's progress was stopped, a relaxed attitude prevailed, indicated by requests from both BLM and Kuna RFD to allow inexperienced personnel to operate the engines on the fire lines.

Other concerns noted that complacency by some BLM personnel regarding the use of personal safety equipment was ignored and overlooked.

After the Red Flag Warning was issued, and when the high winds hit causing the fire line blowup, there were no attempts to verify a safe location of all crews by BLM or Kuna RFD officials in charge. It was found that the BLM Incident Commander and the Kuna Command did not have a face-to-face meeting to discuss and clarify details concerning the shared command process. A few weeks earlier on July 3, Kuna RFD and BLM had successfully fought a wildland fire together, using the United Command approach as described in the Incident Command System.

Equipment and Damage

When the investigators reviewed the equipment that was being used by the Engine 620 crew, they found that the personal protective gear was adequate for fighting structural fires but was not ideal for wildland firefighting. Fire shelters were not available to any of the Kuna RFD crews. That part of the report concluded that it could not be determined with certainty that additional personal protective gear would have altered the outcome of the accident.

Other fire mishap reports show that some firefighters survived similar circumstances when fire shelters were properly deployed outside vehicles. By remaining in the truck, it is believed that the 620 crew were subjected to higher temperatures for a longer time than if they had left the truck and laid on the ground.

"Another factor that may have had dire consequences was that the fire truck had no live fire hose reels, with no way to protect themselves with direct water spray. Had the truck been equipped with such reels, fire shelters, and some water remaining in the tank, it may have provided the crew with enough protection to weather the burnover." (Author's note: After Engine 620 was destroyed by the burnover, photos taken of the truck during the investigation clearly show a hose reel with some unburned hose still on the reel and attached to the left rear side of the truck. The investigation report does not make it clear if this hose reel was operable or not.)

The Kuna brush truck (engine) 620 was a 1954 surplus military six-wheel-drive truck. It was designated as a Type 4X by the US Forest Service and BLM standards. The truck had a gasoline engine, with a 1,500-gallon water tank installed and fitted with a single-stage Hale pump driven by a two-cylinder Wisconsin motor. The pump was used to provide water from the tank to the spray units mounted on the truck's front bumper. The truck had also been fitted with an after-market fiberglass top for the cab.

After 620 was overrun by the wall of fire, the intense heat from the wildfire and the burning truck itself contributed to the complete destruction of the truck. The fiberglass top was completely gone. The tires were burned off with the vehicle sitting directly on the ground, supported only by the rims and axles. There was no support from the springs and shocks due to being warped, and with no flexibility left. The metal on the truck was discolored, and many areas of the tank and cab were warped due to the extreme heat. All the paint had been burned off. All windows and instrument glass were broken and melted.

Any flammable material under the engine hood had been consumed by fire. Later during the investigation as to why the engine had died, it could not be determined why the engine had quit at the critical time due to the fire damage.

Recommendations

The recommendations part of the accident report began with this statement from the investigative team:

"The most important part of this report could very well be the recommendations found in this section. Lessons, however painful, can be learned from the tragedy that occurred at the Point Fire. If the recommendations help to make the difficult job of fighting wildfires safer, then the investigation team's efforts will have been worthwhile."

As expected, one of the most important parts of the recommendations had to do with radio and face-to-face communications during the Point Fire. The investigators determined that a lack of coordination between the BLM IC and the Kuna RFD Command resulted in no clear understanding of who was assigning duties and keeping track of locations of the Kuna RFD units while on the fire. Most of this confusion was a result of not being able to communicate effectively by radio with several of the units.

Some of the recommendations to help alleviate future misunderstandings and confusion during a multi-agency response to a wildfire were covered under the report's Part A.

A. Incident Command and Leadership Factors ...

1. *Where there is a multi-agency response to a single jurisdiction, a single IC should be used. Multiple jurisdictions, such as mixed ownership lands where structure protection is needed, may require a shared command. If there is a question about jurisdictions, agency supervisors must mutually decide on the command structure as soon as they arrive at the fire. Once the decision has been made, the organization in use should be broadcast to all units on the fire as well as dispatch centers.*

Other recommendations under this part covered formal and mutual agreements for fire protection and suppression. It also stressed the need to reaffirm the necessity of briefing crews when fire or weather conditions change significantly.

Since communications played such an important role in this tragic accident, the seven steps to follow, as laid out by the investigators, are listed in their entirety.

B. Communications

Communication, or lack of adequate communication, was a significant factor in this incident. Specifically, common radio communications were not always available to all firefighters on the Point Fire. Instructions and warnings were not always received, and consistent radio contact with engines was not always possible.

Recommendations

1. *BLM and local cooperators should begin to develop and strengthen regional mutual aid communication plans, including radio frequency use and management.*

2. *All cooperating entities should inventory their capabilities to ensure that they are able to communicate on common radio channels. BLM and rural fire departments should consider exchanging radios during multi-agency wildfires.*
3. *The BLM Boise District should provide its Dispatch Center with tape recording capabilities that include automatic time encoding.*
4. *BLM Boise Dispatch should immediately modify its current logging process for documenting radio transmissions by providing a log for each radio dispatch console. Also, BLM Boise Dispatch should institute a separate log specific to each fire whenever possible and limit entries to activities specific to that fire.*
5. *BLM Boise District should better observe National Wildfire Coordinating Group (NWCG) standards for engine designation, identification of individuals and so forth. Use of "clear text" guidelines need to be emphasized. Agency-specific terms, slang, and ten codes need to be eliminated.*
6. *All agencies should reaffirm the need for engines to notify the IC when they reposition themselves, run low on water, and the route they will take to refill.*
7. *Severe weather warnings should be provided to the appropriate city or county dispatch center and the center should broadcast these warnings to those monitoring their frequencies.*

Recommendations for equipment and training under part C stressed standardization of personal protective firefighting gear meeting the National Fire Protection Association Standard #1977 and that all personnel on a wildfire should carry a fire shelter.

Weekly inspections for equipment and personal protective gear by BLM and cooperators should be performed and documented.

Another conspicuous recommendation was that engines must be equipped to distribute water around the entire vehicle for protection in emergencies. It further stated that engines must always retain enough water in the tank to provide protection in an emergency.

For training, the recommendation was that federal agencies, in cooperation with local and state officials, should consider basic wildland firefighting training using the NWCG wildland firefighter training program as a guideline for rural fire departments and other entities participating in wildland firefighting.

The final recommendations dealt with investigation procedures. This was not necessarily related to the Point Fire but covered the investigation of any wildfire. The recommendation stressed the necessity of promptness in beginning the investigation, interviewing witnesses, and preserving evidence.

It was also suggested that an investigation handbook should be developed that would provide guidelines for investigative teams.

(Author's note: Since the Point Fire Accident Investigation report was published, several guideline, pamphlet, and other publications dealing with wildfire investigations have been available.)

Conclusion

As with forest fires, high desert wildfires will continue to increase in frequency and intensity. Rising temperatures, weather pattern changes, longer fire seasons, and urban growth creeping further into the desert areas will increase the potential for disastrous fires like the Point Fire.

While battling these fires, personal safety and the ever-present unexpected dangers to both wildland and structure firefighters will always be a concern. The requirement for further cooperation between multi-agencies will no doubt increase. The demand for more rural volunteer firefighters, and the giving freely of their valuable time to battle these fires, will prevail. Like William Buttram and Joshua Oliver, other brave volunteers will step forward in the defense of their fellow citizens and properties.

In Memory of the Kuna, Idaho, RFD Volunteer Firefighters:
William Buttram Joshua Oliver

CHAPTER EIGHTEEN

Yarnell Fire

The South Canyon Fire on Storm King Mountain would turn out to be the fifth-deadliest wildland fire for firefighters in the United States. After this tragedy, and after all the lessons and tactics learned from this fire, most agencies involved in wildland firefighting improved their training, safety measures, and communications to ensure that this large loss of life would not happen again.

For smokejumper Tony Petrilli, who had survived the South Canyon Fire inside his fire shelter for one and a half hours and witnessed the horrific tragedy, he could not possibly imagine that he would ever be involved in another disaster like the one he had survived. But he would be, nineteen years later, with an even greater loss of life.

Located in Yavapai County, Yarnell, Arizona, is approximately thirty-four miles southwest of Prescott. The 2010 census showed a population of 649. Yarnell and the surrounding area are known for ranching and mining. Before the Yarnell Hill Fire was over, half the town would be destroyed, and nineteen wildland firefighters would perish.

On the afternoon of June 28, 2013, a series of lightning strikes high on a ridge west of Yarnell ignited multiple fires. The fire with the most potential was about one-half acre in steep terrain and inaccessible by vehicles. Seeing very little fire activity, the incident commander decided that due to the late hour and safety concerns of putting firefighters on the fire overnight, they would prepare for full suppression the following morning.

Being on state-managed land, the fire would be under the supervision of the Arizona State Forestry Division with wildland fire suppression assistance from numerous other federal, state, and local agencies and with air support from several locations and agencies.

The Background section of the Yarnell Hill Fire Serious Accident Investigation report describes the conditions facing the firefighters prior to the tragic outcome of the fire:

The Yarnell Hill Fire occurred in west-central Arizona, west of the town of Yarnell along a north–south mountainous ridge with elevations of 4,500 to 6,000 feet. Within the fire area, the terrain varies from steep ridges to nearly flat valley bottoms with numerous rock outcroppings and boulder piles. The dominant vegetation type, chaparral brush, ranged in height from one to ten feet and, in some places, was nearly impenetrable. The Yarnell Hill Fire area had not experienced wildland fire since 1966.

Conditions leading up to the Yarnell Hill Fire consisted of very high to extreme fire danger and extreme drought during a transition to the Southwest's summer monsoon season. During this seasonal transition, temperatures are typically very hot. Relative humidity values remain low but fluctuate as storms become more numerous and cloud cover more prevalent. Winds are highly variable with the highest wind speeds occurring during thunderstorms. These storms can create strong downdrafts, microbursts, outflows, and gust fronts, all of which can affect fire behavior.

The Southwest Coordination Center's Predictive Services issued a Fire Behavior Advisory on June 16, 2013 that discussed critically low fuel moistures and increased fuel loading. On June 25, the National Weather Service (NWS) office in Flagstaff issued an excessive heat watch for Yavapai and northern Gila counties below 4000 feet.

Multiple lightning ignitions occurred from thunderstorm activity on lands southwest of Prescott at about 1700 Phoenix Standard Time (PNT) on Friday, June 28. Of the seven lightning fires discovered, four were on

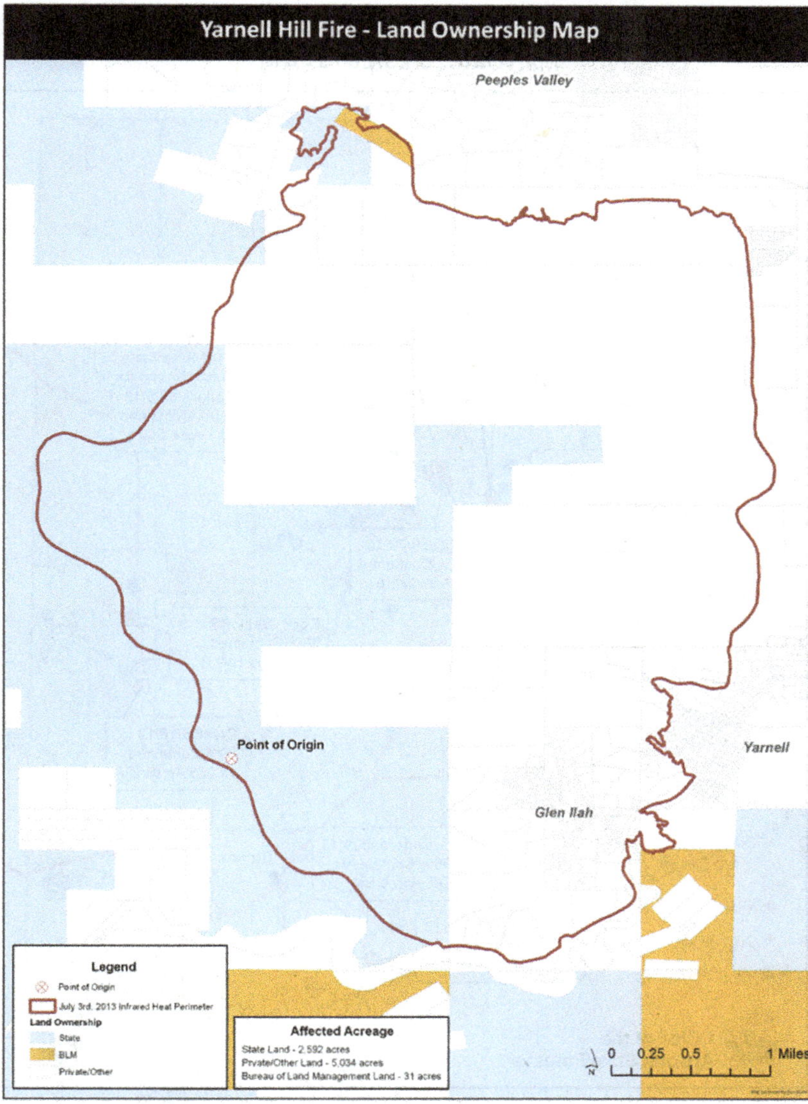

Figure 1 – Yarnell Hill Fire land ownership map. Land within the fire perimeter is a mixture of privately owned, State of Arizona, and BLM-managed land. COURTESY OF ARIZONA STATE FORESTRY DIVISION.

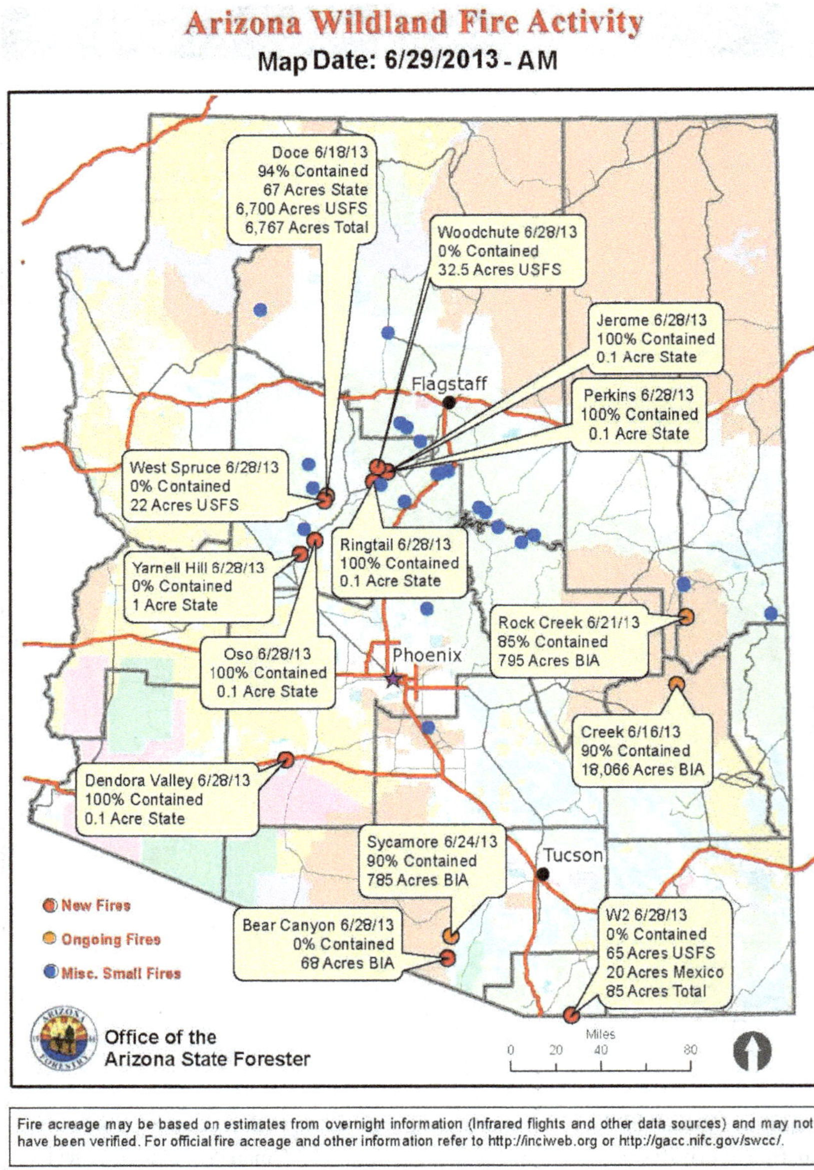

Figure 2 – Arizona Wildland fire activity on June 29, 2013. COURTESY OF ARIZONA STATE FORESTRY DIVISION.

State, private, and adjacent Bureau of Land Management (BLM) lands. The Yarnell Hill Fire was one of these four. Statewide, 37 active fires—four ongoing and 33 new fires—were under management that day. Figure 1, Yarnell Hill Fire Land Ownership Map depicts the boundary of the Yarnell Hill Fire and displays the land ownership within the fire boundary.

The Southwest Area was in Preparedness Level 4 and had eight uncontained large fires, Types 2 and 3 in complexity. These were the Silver, Jaroso, Creek, Doce, Sycamore, Thompson Ridge, Tres Lagunas, and Rock Creek fires. Some precipitation and higher humidity had begun to enter the Southwest in certain places, which assisted agencies in nearing containment on five of the eight fires. Figure 2, Arizona Wildland Fire Activity, shows locations, estimated sizes, percentage contained, and land ownership for the fires burning across the state on June 29.

Resource availability was average for that time of year and planning level. Resources available on June 28 were two Type 1 Incident Management Teams (IMTs), four Type 2 IMTs, three Type 3 IMTs, two Type 1 airtankers, two smokejumper aircraft (2+ loads), approximately ten Single Engine Airtankers (SEATs), two Type 1 helicopters, two Type 2 helicopters, eight Type 1 IHCs (Interagency Hotshot Crews), and Type 2 crew capability. Some of these resources, along with other ordered resources, would eventually be committed to both the Yarnell Hill incident and to the Dean Peak incident a couple of days later.

CHAPTER NINETEEN

Saturday, June 29, 2013

The Arizona Incident Commander (ICT4) and two BLM representatives began planning and coordinating resources to attack the numerous fires in the area. The Yarnell Hill Fire was the most active of the several lightning-ignited fires started the previous day. The ICT4 contacted dispatch, reporting that little smoke was showing and that they planned on dropping retardant to hold the fire until they could get firefighters on the scene. At 06:51, he requested two Single Engine Air Tankers (SEATs). At midmorning, the SEATs began dropping retardant on the south and west flanks of the fire. Around 11:00, a BLM helicopter transported seven firefighters and landed them about a quarter mile from the ridge. One helitack firefighter and six Department of Corrections firefighters then hiked to the fire and began constructing handlines.

The Air Attack aircraft that had been directing and coordinating the retardant drops reported that the retardant was securing the south and west flanks, the north flank was the ridge, and a two-track road secured the east flank. At this time, the fire size was about two acres.

Weather conditions continued to be hot and dry with increasing west–southwest winds that increased fire activity significantly. At 16:10, the incident commander requested that the two SEATs and Air Attack return to the fire. One SEAT and the Air Attack returned to begin retardant drops; the other SEAT was held on standby at Wickenburg Airport for potential new fire starts from active lightning across central Arizona.

The fire jumped the two-track road on the east flank and increased to six acres. The incident commander notified dispatch that they were having problems catching the fire and ordered a Type 1 Heavy Helitanker and a Large Air Tanker (LAT). He also requested a State of Arizona IMT to take charge of the fire the following morning, voicing concerns about potential threats to Peeples Valley and the town of Yarnell if the fire burned to the northeast in the next twenty-four to forty-eight hours.

At 17:42, dispatch informed the incident commander that the Heavy Helitanker and the LAT declined the resource orders because of high winds and severe weather en route from their locations. Dispatch stated that a Very Large Air Tanker (VLAT)—a DC-10 with 11,400-gallon capacity—was available and could take off from an airport unaffected by the weather. After discussing the option with Air Attack, the incident commander declined the VLAT offer and continued to use the SEATs for retardant drops.

The fire continued to grow throughout the evening, now estimated at one hundred acres. The incident commander requested additional resources and notified the Yavapai County Sheriff's Office to prepare for reverse 911 calls in case evacuations became necessary. The resources requested for the next day were fourteen engines, six water tenders, two Type 2 crews, two bulldozers, and numerous aircraft. Also requested were two structure group specialists—one for the north end (Model Creek, Peeples Valley) and one for the south end (Yarnell, Glen Ilah)—and three IHCs.

Dispatch ordered the IHCs through the Southwest Coordination Center (SWCC), one of the nation's interagency Geographic Area Coordination Centers. SWCC filled two of the orders with the Blue Ridge IHC and the Arroyo Grande IHC but advised dispatch to rescind their order for the third crew and fill it internally with the local Granite Mountain IHC. Due to mechanical problems, Arroyo Grande IHC was unable to accept this assignment.

At 19:24, the fire spread in chaparral to the north–northeast with the temperature at 101 degrees Fahrenheit, humidity at 12 percent, and winds of ten miles per hour gusting to twenty out of the south–southwest. Flames were estimated to reach ten to twenty feet with a spread rate of 330 to 660 feet per hour. During the night, thirteen firefighters remained on the hill while other resources remained in the Yarnell and Peeples Valley areas.

CHAPTER TWENTY

Sunday, June 30, 2013

At the Yarnell Fire Station, a briefing was held with the incident commander and others from the previous shift and with the incoming personnel. The Granite Mountain IHC Superintendent Eric Marsh was part of the new team that had recently arrived.

The briefing covered strategy, tactics, weather forecasts, and radio frequencies to be used. Maps were reviewed, and it was noted that the Boulder Springs Ranch would be an excellent safety zone for firefighters if needed. Another concern was keeping the fire away from the town of Yarnell. The fire had now grown to an estimated 300 to 500 acres.

The Fire Management Team discussed the need to establish an anchor point at the heel of the fire on the south end. It was agreed that the Granite Mountain superintendent would assume the duties of Division Supervisor Alpha (DIVS A) and his Assistant Superintendent, Jesse Steed (Granite Mountain Captain), would be in charge of the firefighter crew that would work the south end.

From the Yarnell Hill Fire Serious Accident Investigation report, the establishment and background of the Granite Mountain Hotshots is described:

> *The Prescott Fire Department created a Wildland Division in 2001 to conduct a risk assessment and develop a Vegetation Management Plan for the city. The risk assessment found Prescott to be at risk of catastrophic wildfire. As a result, the Division formed a Fuels Management Crew to create defensible space on private and City-owned property. The 2002 Indian Fire led to an expansion of the crew's duties. In 2004, the Fuels Management Crew evolved into Crew 7, a Type 2 Initial Attack crew that, while continuing with fuels reduction work, responded to wildfires both regionally and nationally. Just before the 2007 season, Crew 7 gained IHC trainee status and became known as the Granite Mountain Hotshots. Following the IHC certification process, Granite Mountain became a certified IHC in 2008.*

During the briefings, and while additional resources continued to arrive at the command post, the fire escalated to the point where it threatened structures in the Model Creek subdivision north of the fire. The sheriff's office issued evacuation notices to the residents of Model Creek and the Double Bar A Ranch. By 13:30, the fire had advanced toward the command post, requiring repositioning of vehicles and personnel.

After the morning briefing, the SPGS1 (Structure Protection Group Supervisor) and the Granite Mountain Hotshot Crew drove through the town of Yarnell, stopping at a property on Sesame Street where the SPGS1 pointed out the Boulder Springs Ranch to the southwest and reminded the crew that the ranch was a "bomb-proof" safety zone. The black (burned-out area) was also suggested as a safety zone.

The hotshots drove down near the end of Sesame Street to a cleared area and parked their crew carriers. Division Supervisor Marsh scouted further up to a point where the road was no longer passable for vehicles and parked his truck. The Hotshot Crew hiked to where the supervisor was and received a briefing, including the report that the weather would be "superhot and windy," structures would be threatened, and that their escape routes would be into the black or back to the crew carriers. The assignment was to establish an anchor point, then determine whether to go direct along the black or to go indirect and burn (backfire) off the two-track road (trail).

The supervisor continued scouting ahead, where after about a forty-five-minute hike along the two-track road, the crew arrived at a potential anchor point. From there, Marsh scouted out the west side of the ridge. A squad of a few crewmembers followed him, working along the fire's edge toward a cold part of the fire where they would establish the anchor point. The fire activity picked up along the east side. The remainder of the crew began burnouts adjacent to the two-track road, keeping pace with the active fire. The supervisor hiked to the top of a ridge arriving at a helispot. A BLM helicopter had dropped off backpack pumps the night before. A helitack crewmember, who had overseen a night crew working the fire and was on board the helicopter headed back to camp, briefed the Hotshot Supervisor by radio. He relayed the weather and fire activity that had taken place during his shift. He estimated the fire's size to be about 500 acres.

Throughout the morning as the temperature began to rise, the fire activity increased. Fire personnel also noted cloud buildups to their north, with one cell becoming very significant and building in size. After operations contacted Marsh by radio, the supervisor confirmed that he could see the buildups through the smoke and that he would continue to monitor the cloud movement.

The Granite Mountain Hotshots continued their burnout along the two-track road. Air Attack was over the fire and discussed tactics and options with the supervisor. Air Attack ordered two SEAT retardant drops directly onto the burnout. This was not what Supervisor Marsh had in mind. He had the Hotshot Crew shift tactics and go direct along the fire's edge building a fire line. While this was going on, the squad on the west side of the ridge completed their handline, tying into the cold black and into the steep, rocky terrain. Eric Marsh felt this was a good anchor, and at about noon, he had the squad rejoin the main crew working on the east side.

Earlier that morning, the Blue Ridge Interagency Hotshot Crew had arrived at the incident command post to receive their assignments and to set their radios to the various frequencies being used on the fire. They proceeded to the Yarnell Fire Station for staging. Operations told them to drive into the fire area and tie in with the SPGS1. The Granite Mountain Supervisor also contacted the Blue Ridge firefighters to discuss the fire. After parking their crew carriers next to the Granite Mountain rigs, Blue Ridge superintendent Brian Frisby and his crew captain unloaded a utility task vehicle (UTV) and continued up the road where they met the SPGS1, who requested a Heavy Equipment Boss to manage a bulldozer that would be used to clear out the two-track road as far as possible and to provide access to prepare for a possible backfire burnout. Blue Ridge assigned a qualified squad leader to the equipment boss job.

The equipment boss directed the dozer to clear a fire line as far as an old, abandoned grader, where they cleared an area around it. Then, they continued pushing the line toward the saddle, near the anchor point established by the Granite Mountain Hotshot Crew. After reaching the saddle, the plan was to return the dozer to clear a firebreak along the two-track road between Sesame Street and Shrine Road. The other members of the Blue Ridge Hotshots remained on standby where the crew carriers were parked.

Around noon, the Blue Mountain superintendent and captain met up with the Granite Mountain superintendent and crew captain on the two-track road. They discussed tactics and agreed that a Granite Mountain firefighter would be utilized as a lookout. This important assignment went to Brendan McDonough. The lookout chose a spot down by the old, abandoned grader, and Granite Mountain Captain Steed agreed that the spot would be a good vantage point. On their way back

Granite Mountain Hotshots early on June 30. PHOTOGRAPH COURTESY OF JOY COLLURA.

to where the rest of the Blue Ridge crew were standing by, the Blue Ridge bosses dropped McDonough off at the old grader. McDonough then hiked about 120 yards to the vantage point and notified Supervisor Marsh that he had "good eyes" on the Granite Mountain Hotshots and the fire. The hotshots responded that they had a good view of the lookout as well as the fire.

The Blue Ridge Hotshot Crew were directed to move their crew carriers to the Shrine of St. Joseph and a youth camp area and prepare to backfire along the dozer line being constructed between Sesame Street and Shrine Road.

Note: The Shrine of St. Joseph of the Mountains in Yarnell was inspired and constructed by the Wasson family in the 1930s during the Great Depression. Over the years, the statues were sculpted and erected along a rocky, uphill path stretching about a quarter mile in length. The Shrine follows the Catholic tradition of Stations of the Cross. The last statue would be at the top of the hill, depicting the Crucifixion of Christ.

The Yarnell Fire reached the Shrine, destroying a gift shop and several other structures. Most statues were covered in ash, but all wooden crosses survived the fire. The statue of Christ on the hilltop survived, but the crossbar and the top of the crucifix had burned away. The outstretched arms of Jesus remained in place, but now nailed to air. The statue remained white and untouched by the fire. The Shrine was restored and repaired after the Yarnell Fire. Today, it remains a popular site for visitors and the faithful.

The fire continued burning north and toward structures in the Peeples Valley area, but the fire was also backing down toward the Granite Mountain crew as well. They continued building the fire line directly along the fire's edge. They built sections of the line and then went back securing the fire line to make sure it was holding. After reaching a rock face anchor point, the crew took a break for lunch. After eating, they worked their way back along the line ensuring that the line was holding. The crew and the fire continued to be observed by McDonough, Marsh,

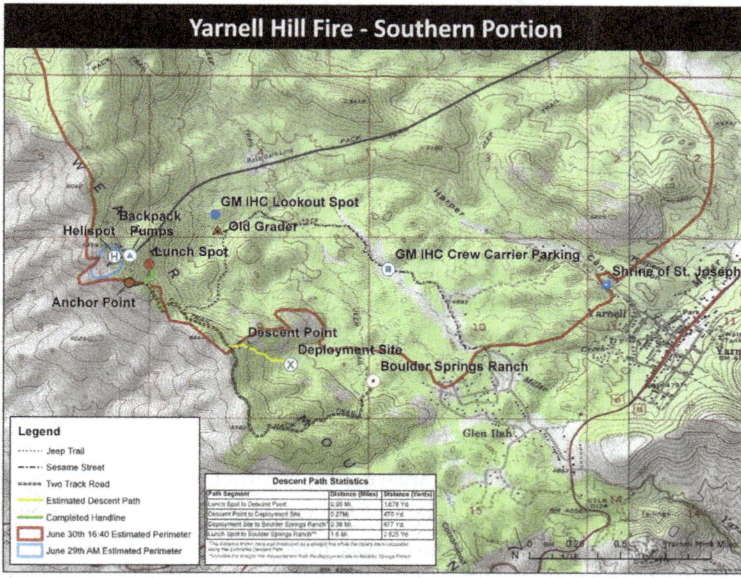

Southern portion of the Yarnell Hill Fire. COURTESY OF ARIZONA STATE FORESTRY DIVISION.

and Steed from different vantage points. As pointed out by the investigation report, the Granite Mountain Lookout had "trigger points" for the crew and for himself in case the fire changed direction. In other words, once the fire or weather became a potential threat for the crew and lookout, they would need to take precautionary actions and move to a more secure area.

Over their radios the lookouts and other firefighters discussed the thunderstorm buildups. Captain Steed relayed that he had seen a few lightning strikes. Around 14:00, the National Weather Service office in Flagstaff, Arizona, relayed to Operations Dispatch and the fire authorities that thunderstorms east of the fire may produce winds and gusts of thirty-five to forty-five miles per hour from the northeast. At 15:26, the Weather Service issued an update on the thunderstorms predicting outflow of winds from the north–northeast with forty- to fifty-mile-per-hour gusts. The Granite Mountain Supervisor contacted the Blue Ridge Hotshot Supervisor and asked to meet up. Blue Ridge Supervisor Frisby headed toward the location in his UTV and heard the second weather update being transmitted. Operations also called the Granite Mountain Supervisor to see if he copied the latest weather update. Marsh affirmed that he received the update and that he was working his way off the ridge. He reported that the winds were getting squirrely at his lookout position.

Air Attack reported that the fire was moving rapidly toward Yarnell and could reach the town in one to two hours. He also advised that the Granite Mountain crew carriers may be in the path of the wildfire. The Air Attack pilot must leave the fire due to flight time and duty time limitations.

At 15:50, McDonough was taking weather observations. Steed contacted the lookout and asked for the weather updates. McDonough noted that the fire to the north was now moving slowly toward his observation point. After scanning the crew's working location and taking more temperature readings and weather observations, he looked back at the fire, which was now building in intensity with an increase and shift in the winds. He notified the Granite Mountain Captain that the fire had reached his trigger point, and he was moving to the open area at the old grader site. Steed acknowledged McDonough's message.

Just as McDonough reached the grader site, Blue Ridge Superintendent Frisby arrived in his Ranger UTV. About then McDonough received a call from Steed, saying, "I've got eyes on you and the fire, and it's making a good push." Frisby used McDonough's radio to speak directly with the Granite Mountain crew since it was already tuned to the intra-crew frequency. He told them that McDonough was with him and safe, and that they were headed back to the crew carriers. Granite Mountain responded that they had "good eyes," and they were in the black. Before reaching the crew carriers, Frisby dropped McDonough off so he could move the Granite Mountain Supervisor's truck. Frisby continued to where his Blue Ridge crew was so he could bring a couple

PHOTOGRAPH TAKEN BY A GRANITE MOUNTAIN HOTSHOT CREWMEMBER ON JUNE 30.

of them back to move the Granite Mountain crew carriers. While en route, the SPGS1 radioed Frisby asking if they still had the option to burn out from the dozer line. The Blue Ridge superintendent told him no. Granite Mountain Superintendent Marsh heard the conversation and transmitted that he agreed and added that he believed the fire was almost to the Granite Mountain vehicles. Marsh also stated, "I want to pass on that we're going to make our way to our escape route."

Attempting to clarify, the Blue Ridge superintendent asked, "You guys are in the black, correct?"

Marsh responded, "Yeah, we're picking our way through the black." He mentioned a road in the bottom and "going out toward the ranch." Frisby thought that the Granite Mountain superintendent was talking about heading northeast, through the black, to one of the ranches in that direction.

"DIVS A, to confirm, you're talking about the road you saw me on with the UTV earlier, in the bottom."

Marsh replied, "Yes, the road I saw you on with the Ranger."

The sheriff's office had issued preevacuation notices to area residents earlier in the day. The Structure Protection Group Superintendent had designated three trigger points for evacuation for northern Yarnell and the Shrine area. The first being a ridge one mile north of town, this would allow a one-hour window to evacuate residents when the fire reached that point. The second trigger point would be for the firefighters' evacuation, and the third trigger point would make sure everyone is out of the area.

A firefighter task force assigned to the Structure Protection Group 1 was constructing a fire line near the youth camp, eastward toward a boulder pile. This line tied in with the dozer line between Shrine Road and Sesame Street that the Blue Ridge Hotshot Crew had been working on since 15:00.

Around 15:30, winds began to increase, gradually shifting direction from southwest to west–northwest and causing an increase in fire activity. The fire was spotting, and heavy ash was falling on the firefighters working near the youth camp. The "Summary of Wind Shifts in the Afternoon" report from the investigation described the winds at the Granite Mountain Hotshot's location. "At the Granite Mountain IHC's location near the anchor point, wind shifts began at approximately 15:50. Before that, the fire was moving generally northeast.

"Around 15:50, the fire shifted to moving southeast and aggressively pushing toward Yarnell. The outflow boundary itself had not arrived yet. It did not hit the southern perimeter of the fire until 16:30. When the outflow boundary hits, winds drastically increase and drive the fire south."

The fire reached the first trigger point and the Structure Protection Superintendent requested that the Yavapai County Sheriff's office order an immediate evacuation for the Yarnell residents. About the same time, drivers arrived at the Shrine with the Granite Mountain crew carriers.

Christopher MacKenzie took this photo at 15:50 on June 30.
PHOTOGRAPH COURTESY OF ARIZONA STATE FORESTRY DIVISION.

Shortly after, the Blue Ridge firefighters loaded up and began leaving the area. Other firefighters remained at the Shrine and in the area. Five to seven minutes later, the fire hit the second trigger point, and the superintendent ordered all firefighters and resources at the youth camp to evacuate. The remaining firefighters in the Shrine area began leaving and moved toward Highway 89. The fire was closing in on them as the last of the crews reached the highway. By this time, it was darkening because of the smoke column. Falling embers were igniting numerous spot fires that rapidly burned together. The firefighters drove south on Highway 89, where they regrouped at the Ranch House Restaurant.

The Air Attack that had to leave earlier because of the pilot's duty limitations had been replaced by another aircraft and Air Attack to assume the duties of directing air retardant drops and coordinating with the firefighters on the fire. The aircraft and personnel assigned to these

One of the VLATs dropping retardant near Yarnell. PHOTOGRAPH BY RICK THAM, COURTESY OF ARIZONA STATE FORESTRY DIVISION.

duties were titled Aerial Supervision Modules. The aircrew assuming responsibility over the Yarnell Fire was identified as ASM2. The Structural Protection Superintendent directed Air Attack to "drop at will" in order to keep the fire from the town.

The increase in fire activity and wind shifts now required that the priorities turn to the protection of Yarnell. Radio traffic was heavy in the cockpit of ASM2, as the pilot directed incoming air tankers on the air-to-air frequency, and the other Air Attack crew member coordinated with operations and the firefighters on the ground.

At approximately 16:00, ASM2 overheard a comment on the radio referencing a crew and a safety zone. ASM2 contacted operations to clarify, "I heard a crew in a safety zone, do we need to call a time out?"

Operations replied, "No, they're in a good place. They're safe and it's Granite Mountain." They discussed flying over to check on the crew, but for now, they thought the crew was safe and in the black. After this

Wade Parker texted this photo at 16:04 on June 30. PHOTOGRAPH COURTESY OF ARIZONA STATE FORESTRY DIVISION.

conversation, Granite Mountain Superintendent Marsh transmitted, "We're going down our escape route to our safety zone."

ASM2 asked, "Is everything okay?"

Marsh responded, "Yes, we're just moving."

ASM2 was in the process of flying a drop, flight path for a VLAT on a west to east direction, and apparently over the Granite Mountain crew. Marsh, seeing the flight, called and calmly said, "[ASM2], Division Alpha, that's exactly what we're looking for. That's where we want the retardant." As ASM2 circled the south end of the fire to line up for a final path for a tanker drop, an overmodulated and static-filled transmission came over the air-to-ground frequency at 16:39: "Breaking in on Arizona 16, Granite Mountain Hotshots, we are in front of the flaming front." Note: Arizona 16 is the Air Guard frequency, an emergency frequency that all aircraft have programmed into their radios and monitor. It appears the Granite Mountain crewmember thought he was breaking in on Arizona 16, but he was on the air-to-ground frequency.

Following this transmission was a very broken transmission, with wind in the microphone: "Air-to-ground 16, Granite Mountain, Air Attack, how do you read?" Due to poor reception, ASM2 received only fragments of these transmissions. Because of the rapid advance of the fire toward Yarnell, Air Attack assumed the broken, unclear radio transmissions were from the structure protection crews calling to request retardant drops. He did not suspect that the calls were from Granite Mountain since they were safe when he talked to them earlier. Operations tried to contact Granite Mountain: "Granite Mountain, Operations on air-to-ground."

Seconds later, Granite Mountain transmitted: "Air Attack, Granite Mountain 7, how do you copy me?"

Other firefighters in other locations heard the radio traffic and could hear chainsaws in the background of the Granite Mountain firefighters' now more urgent transmissions. Concern and confusion about Granite Mountain's location grew, as it was thought that the Granite Mountain Hotshots were safe and in the black. They heard another urgent call: "Air Attack, Granite Mountain 7!"

Air Attack (ASM2), while talking to operations, stated that Granite Mountain's transmissions to him were unclear. And then told the unit calling on air-to-ground to quit yelling.

Operations now believed the unit may be in trouble and told ASM2: "Okay, Granite Mountain 7 sounds like they got some trouble, uh, go ahead and get that, he's trying to get you on the radio, let's go ahead and see what we've got going on."

ASM2 responded: "Okay, copy that. Uh, I'll get with Granite Mountain 7 then."

Moments later, a call from Marsh, DIVS A (sounding calm): "[ASM2], Division Alpha with Granite Mountain."

ASM2: "Okay uh Division Alpha, [ASM2]."

DIVS A (now more urgent): "Yeah, I'm here with Granite Mountain Hotshots, our escape route has been cut off. We are preparing a deployment site and we are burning out around ourselves in the brush and I'll give you a call when we are under the sh—the shelters."

ASM2: "Okay, copy that. So you're on the south side of the fire then?"

DIVS A yelled: "Affirm!"

ASM2: "K, we're gonna bring you the VLAT okay."

Air Attack directed the air tanker to orbit southeast of the fire until they could determine the Granite Mountain crew's location. For the next four minutes, ASM2 tried seven times to make radio contact with Granite Mountain, but to no avail. Helicopter 215KA, just lifting off from the heliport, overheard the radio traffic and contacted ASM2 to help in locating Granite Mountain.

Because of the heavy smoke, the aircraft crews were unable to see the ground. ASM2 continued trying to make contact and told Granite Mountain to listen for the helicopter and let him know when it sounded close to their position. There was no further contact with the Granite Mountain Hotshot Crew.

The investigation team were able to determine the approximate timeline for the Granite Mountain crew's movement and fire shelter deployment:

Granite Mountain Crew Movement, 16:05 to 16:42.

During this period, the Granite Mountain IHC's motivation and path were unknown to other resources on the fire. The best available information (interviews, times, evidence of probable route, and best possible routes) suggests the following:

Around 1605 to 1610, the crew began moving from the flank of the fire where they had been working (the lunch spot area). They traversed the two-track road near the top of the ridge and proceeded southeast along the ridge until they reached a saddle.

> *As they traveled along the ridge, they had a good view of the fire. When they reached the saddle at the logical spot to descend, they had a direct and clear view of the Boulder Springs Ranch but they rapidly lost their view of the fire. The Ranch appears to be very close and readily accessible. The view is deceptive, however, because after an initial descent, the slope quickly drops off. The route to the Ranch is arduous, strewn with boulders and covered with thick chaparral brush. According to one local, the terrain in the area is not difficult but it is time consuming.*
>
> *Granite Mountain IHC worked their way down the slope through the boulders and brush until the flaming front cut them off.*

While the Granite Mountain crew were working their way toward the safety zone at the ranch, the thunderstorms and outflow of winds were increasing in speed and intensity. Winds were blowing east–southeast as they reached the active fire. There were two heads of the fire moving southward at an increasing rate, creating a smoke plume that rose more than 31,500 feet in height. As the outflow reached the southern perimeter, it pushed the fire to the main ridgeline to the south and into the south end of Yarnell. By 16:48, the smoke plume reached 40,000 feet in height.

After Granite Mountain radioed that they were preparing to deploy their fire shelters, operations and resources on the fire began immediate preparations for search and rescue of the trapped firefighters. Medical personnel, evacuation helicopters, and ambulances were requested for immediate help. The Blue Ridge Interagency Hotshot Crew and other firefighters began a ground search for the Granite Mountain firefighters.

Helicopter Ranger 58, belonging to the Arizona Department of Public Safety and assigned to the fire, joined ASM2 and the crews in search of the Granite Mountain Hotshots. They began their aerial search at the last known location. Heavy smoke limited the helicopter crew's search area.

After a while, the smoke began to clear, and Ranger 58 spotted the Boulder Springs Ranch. The helicopter crew recalled earlier hearing the communications from Granite Mountain about heading for the ranch. Flying in that direction, almost an hour into the search, they located the shelters about a mile south-southeast of Granite Mountain's last known location.

PHOTOGRAPH COURTESY OF THE ARIZONA DEPARTMENT OF FORESTRY.

Unable to find a suitable landing spot close by, the pilot landed about 500 yards from the shelters. The paramedic hiked to the deployment site, and, at 18:35, confirmed that none of the Granite Mountain firefighters survived the fire. He noted that the nineteen crewmembers were in various stages of deploying their shelters when the fire overtook them. They were a third of a mile west of the ranch.

The fire investigator's summary states:

This tragedy occurred when the Granite Mountain IHC was traveling through an unburned area toward a safety zone when a rapidly advancing fire of great intensity overtook them. The fire's extreme speed of 10 to 12 miles per hour eliminated any opportunity for the crew to reach the safety zone or return up to the canyon rim. The crew had less than two minutes to improve a shelter deployment site by using chain saws and burning out. The crew were deploying their fire shelters close together in a small area when the fire overtook them. The deployment site in the box canyon was not survivable because heavy brush caused direct flame contact, and temperatures exceeded 2000°F as the fire swept through the site.

The Serious Accident Investigation Team was assembled almost immediately after the tragic events of the Yarnell Hill Fire. The team consisted of local, state, and federal agencies. Members of the team were experts in all aspects of the investigation. Among the experts examining equipment and the fire shelters was Tony Petrilli, an Equipment Specialist from the USFS Missoula Technology and Development Center.

Petrilli was a smokejumper who had survived the South Canyon Fire, spending one and a half hours inside his deployed fire shelter nineteen years earlier. At the time of the Yarnell Hill Fire, Petrilli was leading a team to redesign and improve fire shelters at the US Forest Service base in Missoula, Montana.

The tragic loss of nineteen firefighters made the Yarnell Hill Fire the third-deadliest wildland fire in the US, surpassed only by the Griffin Park Fire in 1933 and the deadliest wildland fire on record, the Devil's Broom Fire in 1910.

Photos, illustrations, and sketches are from the Yarnell Hill Fire Serious Accident Investigation, dated September 23, 2013, unless otherwise noted.

In Memory of the Granite Mountain Hotshots:

Andrew S. Ashcraft
Travis C. Carter
Christopher A. MacKenzie
Grant Q. McKee
Scott D. Norris
John J. Percin, Jr.
Jesse J. Steed
Travis Turbyfill
Clayton T. Whitted
Garrett Zuppiger
Robert E. Caldwell
Dustin J. DeFord
Eric S. Marsh
Sean M. Misner
Wade S. Parker
Anthony M. Rose
Joe B. Thurston
William H. Warneke
Kevin J. Woyjeck

The top ten US wildfires for loss of wildland firefighters:

Devil's Broom, St. Joe Valley, ID. August 20, 1910. 78 fatalities.

Griffith Park Fire, Los Angeles, CA. October 3, 1933. 29 fatalities.

Yarnell Hill Fire, Yarnell, AZ. June 30, 2013. 19 fatalities.

Rattlesnake Fire, Willows, CA. July 9, 1953. 15 fatalities.

Blackwater Forest Fire, Shoshone National Forest, WY. August 21, 1937. 15 fatalities.

South Canyon Fire, Glenwood Springs, CO. July 6, 1994. 14 fatalities.

Mann Gulch Fire, Helena, MT. August 5, 1949. 13 fatalities.

Loop Fire, Los Angeles, CA. November 1, 1966. 12 fatalities.

Hauser Canyon Fire, Cleveland National Forest, CA. October 1, 1943. 11 fatalities.

Inaja Fire, Cleveland National Forest, CA. November 24, 1956. 11 fatalities.

Information courtesy of National Fire Protection Association.

Resources

Arizona State Forestry Division. Yarnell Hill Fire Serious Accident Investigation Report. 2013. https://docs.google.com/file/d/0B36DIycSgbzWSUtjNkl1Z2ROT0k/edit?resourcekey=0-b1VknEtrot7bm6bA7f5M9g

Forest Service - United States Department of Agriculture. Accident Report DC-3 Aircrash Nezperce National Forest, Idaho. 1979.

Idaho U.S. District Court. Findings of Fact. Civil Case No. 96-0324-S-BLW. https://www.coloradofirecamp.com/point-fire/decision-factual.htm

Occupational Safety and Health Administration (OSHA). The Occupational Safety and Health Administration's Investigation of the South Canyon Fire. 1995. https://www.nwcg.gov/sites/default/files/wfldp/docs/sr-sc-osha.pdf

South Canyon Fire Accident Investigation Team. Report of the South Canyon Fire Accident Investigation Team. 1994. https://archive.org/details/southcanyonfirei14sout/page/n1/mode/2upview=theater

U.S. Department of the Interior, Bureau of Land Management. Point Fire Accident Investigation. 1995. https://www.wildfirelessons.net/HigherLogic/System/DownloadDocumentFile.ashx?DocumentFileKey=1192fe3c-3116-4465-9255-e5b52ff47767&forceDialog=0

About the Author

Robert W. Sisk is a retired professional helicopter pilot with 14,000 hours of flight time. Sisk is a combat veteran of the Vietnam War, having flown 1,059 combat hours while piloting assault helicopters. Of the 14,000 flight hours, over 5,000 hours were flown as an aerial firefighter battling wildfires in the US western and southwestern states, and the state of Alaska.

Previous literary works include the book *Wings for the Valiant*, as well as articles published in *Soldier of Fortune* magazine, *Saga* magazine, and *Survive* magazine.

Robert resides on a ranch in southwestern Idaho, where he enjoys his horses and rural living.

Robert W. Sisk with a Sikorsky S-61 helicopter.